Also available from Kogan Page

Business Basics Series

A full list is available from the publisher.
Telephone 071-278 or 0433 or fax 071-837 6348.

BUDGETING
FOR BUSINESS

BUDGETING
FOR BUSINESS

LEON HOPKINS

KOGAN
PAGE

First published in 1994

Kogan Page Limited
120 Pentonville Road
London N1 9JN

British Library Cataloguing in Publication Data

A CIP record for this book is available from the British Library.

ISBN 0-7494-1042-6

Typeset by Books Unlimited (Nottm), Sutton-in-Ashfield, Notts.
NG17 1AL.
Printed and bound in Great Britain by Clays Ltd, St Ives plc.

Contents

Preface

Governments do it, households do it, and every business ought to do it.

Budgeting is a discipline that shows what is possible, what is not, and one which later allows progress towards what is feasible to be measured and managed.

It is both part of the planning process and an essential ingredient in management control.

The principles involved are easy enough – estimate what you are going to sell, calculate what you need to buy or make to support those sales, and think about the labour and machinery needed to run the business. Put money values on it all, review the results and hone the plans accordingly. The result is your expected profit – or loss.

But there is no common format to apply, no official form to fill in, no published list to check off so you can be sure nothing has been omitted. And there are many estimations and assumptions to be made.

Getting the best out of the technique means adopting a logical and methodical approach to structuring and compiling budgets so that they are tailored to the idiosyncrasies of the business and the style and priorities of its managers.

This book aims to give an overview of the budgeting process, showing why it is important, what are its many uses, and how to milk the most benefit. Principles of compilation and presentation are discussed and ways of identifying and dealing with weaknesses, assumptions and uncertainties suggested.

Budgets are certain to be wrong. But without them businesses would be floundering, travelling in hope rather than expectation, and in an uncertain direction. With them they are able to progress with the confidence of having the route planned in advance and being able to tick off the milestones along the way.

1. Certainty of uncertainty

There is nothing so certain as that the future is uncertain. If it were not so there would be no percentages to play, no point in taking risks, however small, and no point in being in business.

Businesses earn profits by accepting risks, by launching new products, by investing in design and new technology, by stocking up to meet expected demand, and a host of other ways. They do it because there is a pay-back. The reward, if they get it right, will be a return on investment that is more than they could earn by simply keeping money in a deposit or building society account, and more than they have to pay by way of interest on the money they borrow.

If they get it wrong, of course, there may be no rewards at all, only unpaid bills to be settled.

Stacking the odds

Taking a risk is one thing. Taking a gamble is another.

The punter playing roulette is gambling – the odds are stacked against him.

The casino accepting his bets is in business. It has worked out the odds in its favour. It knows that some gamblers will win but that most will lose. It can calculate its average net take per hour, per day, per week and per year. By the same token it can estimate its expenses and hence its likely annual profit.

The outcome is not certain, but unless there is something seriously wrong with its estimations, the variations will not depend upon the spin of a wheel. They will fluctuate with membership and attendance levels, with staffing and upkeep costs. The swings are unlikely to be sudden and uncontrolled. And if management is on the ball, they can be corrected or accommodated in good time.

If being in business is to be more than a gamble – and there will be few backers for long shot riches-or-ruins ventures – owners, financiers and managers need to know that they have a reasonable chance of succeeding. They need to have the comfort of a reliable assessment of the opportunities, risks and the dangers that lie waiting.

In the shorter term this comes in the form of a budget. Budgets are the best estimate of what will happen, in financial terms, over the coming months.

Certain to be wrong

They are certain to be wrong. So why bother?

There are a number of reasons.

First, the very act of preparing annual budgets is itself useful, in most cases essential.

Most businesses are not simply ventures that depend on a handful of transactions. They are complicated. Whether they thrive or dive rests on the outcome of many thousands of transactions, untold numbers of decisions. And the way these deeds impinge upon each other can have unexpected consequences that are unlikely to be guessed at.

Budget preparation makes businesses quantify the effects of likely trading levels and show how sales, purchases, manufacturing, employment expectations and plans interact.

It effectively stacks the odds in favour of the business by allowing it to identify and cut out those activities that are too much of a gamble, that offer too low a return for the risks involved, or that are simply not feasible.

Budget preparation provides the basis of reconciling or revising claims from different parts of the business for use of its resources.

'If we invest in an extra sales person sales will go up, but to do it we will have to delay buying that new bit of plant which means that there will be more breakdowns and repair costs will go up.' Sometimes the overall results will be surprising, sometimes unacceptable. Usually the first draft of a budget is not the last. Setting down the likely outcome will suggest ways of improving results, or perhaps identify areas where cuts can or should be made.

Demonstrating viability

Just as importantly, once finalised, budgets allow the business to demonstrate to backers that its future is not on a knife edge and when and how they can expect to be repaid, and to staff what is expected of them.

Budgets are a blueprint for the year that show what resources will be needed when. If sales are expected to go up in the autumn, stock has to be built up through increased production in the summer, which means recruiting extra machinists in the spring, ordering special materials that come from abroad at Christmas, and having cash in the bank to fund the operation throughout.

Means of control

Finally, budgets are a means of control, an aid to management. By splitting the business into cost or profit centres, budgets in fact deal out responsibilities. Budget holders know what they may spend and what not, what they must make and what is not good enough. They know they will be judged in part by how well they have kept within the limits of the budgets that they have played a part in setting.

Comparison of actual results with those previously budgeted will always throw up differences. Differences mean that things are not going according to plan, perhaps by a little, perhaps by a lot. Estimates of how uncertainties would turn out must have been inaccurate. Next time the process can be refined but besides such lessons there are more immediate gains.

MADEUP ENGINEERING COMPANY

Trading results – March

	March			Year to date		
Sales:	Actual £000	Budget £000	Variance £000	Actual £000	Budget £000	Variance £000
Pump cases	129	117	12	348	335	13
Piston rods	70	86	(16)	224	266	(42)
Total	199	203	(4)	572	601	(29)
Production costs:						
Pump cases	63	62	(1)	174	177	3
Piston rods	32	43	11	96	133	37
Total	95	105	10	270	310	40
Manufacturing margin	104 52%	98 48%	6	302 53%	291 48%	11
Other costs:						
Sales and marketing	45	30	(15)	115	90	(25)
Distribution	18	17	(1)	47	54	7
Adminstration	32	30	(2)	110	90	(20)
Total	95	77	(18)	272	234	(38)
Net margin	9	21	(12)	30	57	(27)

Madeup Engineering's March management accounts show that it is not doing as well as budgeted. Although sales are down – because piston rods have not sold as well as forecast – this shortfall has been more than made good by savings in production costs. But sales and marketing and administration costs are running out of control. Examination of the more detailed departmental budgets will pinpoint the problem further.

Figure 1.1 *Budgets are part of the control weaponry available to managers. Comparing actual results with previously set budgets means that deviations from course can be quickly spotted, put right or accommodated.*

Action needed

Pinpointing the cause of those differences will show whether action is needed, and if so what. Things can be put right before it is too late.

To be used to most effect as part of the management control system, budgets must be broken down into digestible time bites that coordinate with management accounting periods. Typically budgets will be divided into months so that a running check can be kept throughout the year.

Of course, budgets are no use unless based on serious assessment of what is likely to happen. The broader based the figures, the less useful they are likely to be.

Wild guesses

The fact that a wild guess does not prove accurate is hardly likely to provide any insight worth having – except about the degree of budgeting responsibility that should be given to the person making the guess.

So budgets need to be based on reasonable assumptions – that are clearly stated so everybody knows when they no longer hold true – and calculations that stand up to scrutiny.

This means working from the bottom up. Sales budgets should be the result of adding together the individual budgets of each salesperson, purchases, the total of each buyer's budget, and so on.

Involving everybody with responsibility for earning or spending money helps to build unity of purpose and understanding of what the business is about. But there are dangers in allowing individuals to set their own budgets without question or justification.

On the one hand, the natural exuberance of some people may lead to undue optimism on, say, sales. On the other, a natural caution may cause others to set themselves budgets that they know can be achieved easily.

Those responsible for spending may put the figure higher than strictly necessary for fear that, once cut, their budget will never be restored. At the end of the year they will make sure that every penny is spent for the same reason.

14 Budgeting for business

MADEUP ENGINEERING COMPANY

Sales budget – first quarter
John Adams : Midlands area – pump cases

Customer		Jan	Feb	Mar	Total
Ace Pumps	Quantity	2,000	2,000	2,000	6,000
	Price	£2.00	£2.00	£2.00	£2.00
	Sales value	£4,000	£4,000	£4,000	£12,000
	Value last year	£3,300	£3,300	£3,300	£9,900
Defoe Water	Quantity	1,800	3,600	5,400	10,800
and Gas	Price	£1.80	£1.65	£1.65	£1.675
	Sales value	£3,240	£5,940	£8,910	£18,090
	Value last year	£1,800	£3,600	£3,600	£9,000
Lixstowe	Quantity	4,500	5,000	4,500	14,000
Heaters	Price	£1.80	£1.80	£1.80	£1.80
	Sales value	£8,100	£9,000	£8,100	£25,200
	Value last year	£8,000	£8,900	£8,000	£24,900
Syke and	Quantity	4,200	14,400	1,400	20,000
Wexford Eng	Price	£1.70	£0.77	£2.10	£1.06
	Sales value	£7,140	£11,090	£2,940	£21,170
	Value last year	£6,500	£6,500	£10,000	£23,000
Total	Quantity	12,500	25,000	13,300	50,800
	Price	£1.80	£1.20	£1.80	£1.53
	Sales value	£22,480	£30,030	£23,950	£76,460
	Value last year	£19,600	£22,300	£24,900	£66,800
List price		£2.10	£2.10	£2.10	£2.10
% of list price achieved		86%	57%	86%	73%
% Increase (decrease) over last year		14.7%	34.7%	(3.8%)	14.5%

Madeup Engineering's sales budgeting process begins with each sales-person estimating likely sales for the period ahead, in this case done on a customer-by-customer basis. Adding information about last year provides a yardstick that indicates whether the figures appear realistic, over-optimistic or pessimistic. In this case the salesperson, John Adams, will be asked why he estimates sales to Defoe Water and Gas to be on an upward trend and why Syke and Wexford Engineering is expected to make abnormally high orders in February, although the firm also increased its orders in March last year.

John Adams' figures will next be consolidated with those of other sales-people to give a national total sales budget for pump case sales.

Figure 1.2 *Budgeting is a bottom-up process, working from the particular to the global. A starting place for the sales budget is each individual sales person's estimate for the coming year.*

In truth budgets that are targets rather than best estimates, or that represent the minimum achievable, are of not much more use than the wild guess.

Being over budget can be just as disastrous as being under budget.

It is no good earning unexpected (except by the salesperson concerned), mega orders if fulfilling those orders causes strain on production facilities, increased wages through unplanned overtime and severe cash flow problems.

This is partly why the budget-setting process itself is so important as a means of questioning and review, gaining understanding, setting priorities and apportioning resources.

Businesses are a whole and operate best and most efficiently when moving forward in a coordinated way.

This is no easy task. Without a well-prepared budget it will often be an impossible task that leaves the business jumping from one crisis to another.

2. Matters of detail

There are laws which say what must be shown in annual company accounts.

These are the year end financial statements prepared for external consumption – for shareholders, the tax inspector and the bank manager. They are backward looking documents recording what has gone on in the last year. They are not designed to be used for managing the business, for keeping it on the financial straight and narrow during the course of the year.

For that task something different is required, something more immediate and more detailed in key areas.

Management accounts are a trading necessity rather than a legal requirement. Their frequency, format and content are a matter of management choice. There are some ground rules, of course. The figures must be available frequently and quickly enough to allow remedial action to be taken when necessary. And there must be some relation to the financial year end figures so that the cumulative management accounting numbers can be reconciled to the eventual financial accounts.

Consistency of treatment

Businesses have got themselves into scrapes by not paying enough attention to the relationship between financial and management accounts, so that what appeared to be a successful trading period according to the management accounts turned out to be far from successful when year end adjustments were taken into account.

This means that there must be reasonable consistency of accounting treatments. So while the speed of management accounting might mean that they include more estimates than financial accounts, they should not, for example, be based on a different basis of stock valuation than the year end accounts.

But it does not mean that management accounts need necessarily be as comprehensive as financial accounts. In many cases they are considerably more comprehensive.

Degree of complexity

This all depends on the business, its degree of complexity and managers' judgement of what comprise the key indicators.

Sales achieved might be the only figure worth looking at in a small trading company dealing in a single product where, apart from purchases of goods for resale, costs do not vary from week to week.

In most cases it is not that simple. Sales will certainly be important, but the mix of products sold and the price achieved must be considered too. Raw material costs, wage costs, distribution and selling costs and other overheads will also be important.

How much detail is reported is a matter of management choice. Too much detail is time consuming to produce and likely to be confusing into the bargain; too little detail and key areas could be ignored or overlooked.

The important thing to remember is that management accounting is a tool to be used and not an end in itself. It would be pointless and wasteful to produce management accounts in more detail than is useful in understanding and controlling the business.

Management accounting is itself something that needs to be costed, appraised for its worth, budgeted and controlled.

Of course, not everybody needs to see every part of the management accounts – indeed, it is probably better that they don't. Depending on company attitude, size and style, everybody might be told how the company is doing overall. But there is probably no need to tell salespeople such details as production staff overtime costs, or production people, salespeople's travelling expenses.

18   Budgeting for business

MADEUP ENGINEERING COMPANY
Organisation chart

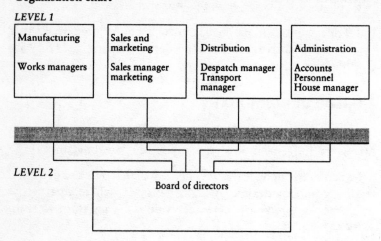

Madeup Engineering is a small engineering company with two plants, one making pump casings, the other piston rods. Each has a separate works manager. The sales team is headed by a sales manager with other advertising and promotion the responsibility of the sales and marketing director. Other departmental heads include a transport manager, despatch manager, personnel manager and accountant.

At departmental level (level 1 above) these managers budget for their own departments. They receive management accounts which show in detail how they have met their own budgets, and also a summary sheet showing how the company is doing as a whole.

There are five directors, one heading each of the four divisions, plus a managing director. They agree the overall budgets, and see and monitor management accounts covering all four divisions, concentrating their attention on overall results and variances from the budget.

Figure 2.1 *Budgets and management accounts should be similar if not identical in structure and reflect management responsibilities within the business. But not every manager will need to see the entire package of management accounts.*

MADEUP ENGINEERING COMPANY
Sales budget – first quarter
Pump cases

Salesperson		Jan	Feb	Mar	Total
John Adams (Midlands)					
	Quantity	12,500	25,000	13,300	50,800
	Price	£1.80	£1.20	£1.80	£1.53
	Sales value	£22,480	£30,030	£23,950	£76,460
	Value last year	£19,600	£22,300	£24,900	£66,800
Ken Allen (North)					
	Quantity	15,100	15,000	15,100	45,200
	Price	£2.10	£2.10	£2.10	£2.10
	Sales value	£31,710	£31,500	£31,710	£94,920
	Value last year	£30,300	£29,000	£30,200	£89,500
Hugh Cruikshank (Export)					
	Quantity	15,400	32,500	30,400	78,300
	Price	£1.60	£1.43	£1.46	£1.47
	Sales value	£24,640	£46,475	£44,385	£115,500
	Value last year	£30,000	£37,700	£35,300	£103,000
David Hardy (South)					
	Quantity	8,000	6,700	8,000	22,700
	Price	£2.10	£2.10	£2.10	£2.10
	Sales value	£16,800	£14,070	£16,800	£47,670
	Value last year	£16,600	£15,000	£16,500	£48,100
Total	Quantity	51,000	79,200	66,800	197,000
	Price	£1.87	£1.54	£1.75	£1.70
	Sales value	£95,630	£122,075	£116,845	£334,550
	Value last year	£96,500	£104,000	£106,900	£307,400
List price		£2.10	£2.10	£2.10	£2.10
% of list price achieved		89%	73%	83%	81%
% Increase (decrease) over last year		(1%)	17.5%	9.4%	9.0%

Madeup Engineering's sales manager budgets for the expected sales for each salesman and each product that is his responsibility. Here he has compiled the Pump cases sales budget by consolidating the budgets for each individual salesperson.

Figure 2.2 *At divisional level managers would be fully involved in budgeting for and monitoring the results for which they are given responsibility.*

The governing principle must be that managers receive the results for that part of the business for which they are held responsible.

This indicates some sort of reporting hierarchy. So departmental managers receive details of their part of the operation; further up the line more senior managers receive more comprehensive figures, giving them an overall picture of that larger part of the business for which they are responsible, and so on up the line.

Concentrating on exceptions

The most senior managers would have overall figures for the business backed up by the more detailed statements when needed. In other words the reporting system would mirror the management structure of the business.

Budgeting works in a similar way.

Once set, budgets become an important part of the management accounting process. They are the yardstick against which quarterly, monthly, weekly or even daily results are assessed. They enable managers to measure their success or otherwise against the criteria that they have played a part in setting for themselves. And, most importantly, they enable managers to manage efficiently by concentrating on the exceptions, those variances from budget where something is not working out as expected.

It follows that the relationship between the format of budgets and management accounts is very close.

Both management accounts and budgets reflect responsibilities. To be able to make comparisons, there should be a budgeted figure for every line of the management accounts, for each reporting period, whether it be quarterly, monthly or weekly.

The budgets at the start of a period will therefore be the expected management accounts at the end of the period.

3. Budget breakdown

One of the benefits of budgets is that they show a 'complete picture', how different parts of a business interact to provide a result.

This, of course, is an impossible ideal. The world is not that simple. Chaos theorists talk about the movement of a butterfly in Japan affecting the weather in Idaho. Quantum theory shows that no experiment is untainted by the presence of the experimenter.

In short, no business operates in isolation from its environment. So the 'whole picture', even if painted in the finest detail, can never tell the whole story. Neither can that snapshot show the only story.

Like pictures, budgets can be approached from different angles, illustrate different aspects. And like photographs, they are restricted by technical and physical edges.

In many ways this makes them more, rather than less, useful – provided the user is aware of the limitations. There is, after all, only so much information that can be taken in at once. Too much and the senses are swamped; the message becomes meaningless. A photograph taken across the winning line of a race is much more useful for measuring the result than a panoramic view of the stadium in which it is being staged, taken from an airship.

The best that can be done

But what this means is that budgeting is a compromise. It involves using a certain amount of creative licence and making the best of what can be achieved.

That best is a coordinated package in which different statements articulate.

So the sales budget includes a sales figure in which the units sold marry with the number of units used in the production budget and with the cash coming into the business – adjusted for credit periods, of course – shown in the cash flow statement. Production wages are calculated on the basis of the hours needed to manufacture budgeted output, which in turn tie in with the machine hours available, and so on.

As all the figures are interdependent, the budgeting process itself has to be coordinated, and calculations have to have a starting point.

The usual process is to start with expected sales, then to work out and cost what has to be bought in and made to service those sales.

Alongside, repairs and maintenance budgets will be prepared that take into account the level of expected use of plant and machinery and buildings and necessary replacements and increases in capacity.

Also the cost of activities not directly related to sales or output – 'overheads' such as the accounts department – will have to be estimated.

The elements are not necessarily distinct in a physical sense. Salespeople may share an office with accounts people, or with salespeople from other departments, or even be 'shared' between departments.

Rather, the elements to the budget represent control.

Sales first

The sales budget is the starting point, since the revenue coming into the business is its driving force. There is no point making the finest, best, most highly regarded products if they can't be sold.

There lies the route to ruin.

So salespeople, often the most optimistic of individuals, must be asked to say not what is possible but what is highly probable, and when.

On these predictions all else rests. But in many ways arriving at a sales budget is the easy part.

Cost conscious

Calculating the cost of sales, in all but the simplest of businesses, is not as simple as it might seem.

If you are running a shop, the direct cost of items sold – those costs that vary in direct proportion to sales – is what the wholesaler charges you.

Start providing services or manufacturing things and it becomes more complicated. Costs will vary according to the level of activity. The reason is that some costs – indirect costs – do not go up and down with sales.

So if a business pays £100,000 a year rent for a factory capable of producing 100,000 pumps a year, the 'rent' element of production costs could be £1 per pump. But if sales are down and the factory is working at only half capacity the rent still has to be paid. The 'rent' element of production costs therefore becomes £2 per pump.

Pricing decisions

Here we enter the realms of costing theory and pricing policy. Would it be better to lower the price of the pumps to increase sales, and hence lower those indirect unit costs?

One way of looking at it is that as long as the sales price is more than the direct or variable costs, a 'contribution' is being earned to pay for those indirect or fixed costs.

And certainly, tactical or long-term strategy considerations apart – for example, to get a foothold in a particularly promising market – there can be no justification for setting sales prices below direct costs.

24 Budgeting for business

In the short term, when conditions are tough, businesses might decide that it is better to accept less than full recovery of indirect costs.

But this is a bit like the paradox of the tortoise and the hare. If the tortoise, which has a 100-yard start, moves ten yards when the hare moves 100 yards, and one yard when the hare moves ten, and three inches when the hare moves 30, and so on, how can the hare ever catch the tortoise?

But we know from experience that it does, that the lines cross.

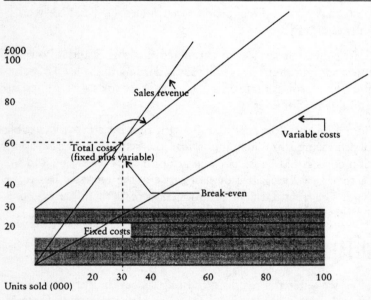

Another Company has fixed costs of £30,000 a year made up of such items as rent and rates, depreciation and leasing charges, and variable costs of £1 a unit. Setting the sales price at or below the variable cost would mean that total costs would never be covered. Any sales at more than £1 a unit would yield a contribution to fixed costs although the lower the margin, the higher the sales volume would need to be to recover all costs. In this instance Another Company has decided to set its sales price at £2 per unit giving a break-even point – where all costs are recovered – of 30,000 units (when sales revenue and total costs both equal £60,000), a sales level which Another Company's sales director is certain can be bettered.

Figure 3.1 *Another Company: pricing policy – a margin for error*

Likewise, a pricing policy based on variable costs, and ignoring indirect costs, would lead any business to be caught out eventually.

In the longer term, if the business is to survive, all those margins must tot up to at least the total of indirect costs.

Full recovery

The point of all this is that every business has indirect costs of some kind – overheads that must be met from income. And these must be included within budgets, preferably in a way which reflects the management view of how they will be recovered.

Budgets are not 'targets' but they do represent the business goalposts. How they are constructed will affect the way individuals react and how the business is run.

Take the example of the shop mentioned above. Even shops have overheads to recover.

If it were thought worthwhile budgets could be prepared for each product line with overheads allocated to each, so that, say, finance costs were shared out according to the amount of money tied up in stock, rent and rates according to the floor area needed to hold stocks of, and to display, each line.

Such sharing out of costs would certainly show the relative 'profit' from each line in a different light to a straight comparison of retail and wholesale price. Some lines would be pushed harder than previously, some played down.

Fair shares

There is no correct way of allocating overheads. The method used should reflect the degree of sophistication that is worthwhile, the objectives and style of management of the company.

All overheads might be lumped together and simply parcelled out in proportion to, say, turnover on the grounds that any attempt at further sophistication would simply be a waste of time and effort.

More typically, in businesses of any size, an attempt is made to match the method of allocation to the type of cost.

So the cost of a personnel department might be allocated according to the number of employees, the cost of rent and rates according to floor space occupied, or the cost of the accounts department according to size of turnover.

Responsible people

Budgets both reflect and distribute responsibilities.

In a business of any size each manager at each level is likely to have his or her own budget. Each may be a 'cost centre' or a 'profit centre' budget. The difference is that the first deals only with a level of expenditure – say, the stationery budget. The second deals instead with the result of the operations of that department: there is both income and expenditure and the budget shows – and the manager is responsible for achieving – the expected margin between the two.

Probably a number of cost and revenue budgets will combine to produce a results budget for each profit centre.

So the manager of a division with its own sales team and production facilities would be given responsibility for earning a given profit. His or her sales manager would have responsibility for achieving an expected level of revenue and the production manager for producing the products sold at the budgeted cost.

So in the case of Another Company (see Figure 3.2), each of its three divisions – printing, engineering and electronics – is treated as a profit centre, virtually as a separate business. And within the profit centre there are various cost centres – for example, 'Production' and 'Delivery and transport'.

The difference between a profit centre and an entirely separate business is that the profit centre will be bound by overall company policy and will not have a free hand in every aspect of its operations.

Budgeted trading – next year

Production

	Divisions				Company
	Printing	Engineering	Electronics	Head office	
	£000	£000	£000	£000	£000
Materials	85	135	25		245
Wages	65	85	105		255
Repairs and maintenance	15	5	9		29
Depreciation	10	5	6		21
Total	175	230	145		550

Delivery and transport costs

	Divisions				Company
	Printing	Engineering	Electronics	Head office	
	£000	£000	£000	£000	£000
Drivers' wages	15	25	14		54
Fuel	5	8	5		18
Tax and insurance	3	4	2		9
Vehicle maintenance	2	3	6		11
Vehicle depreciation	10	15	8		33
Total	35	55	35		125

Overall trading

	Divisions				Company
	Printing	Engineering	Electronics	Head office	
	£000	£000	£000	£000	£000
Sales	300	450	265		1,015
Production costs	175	230	145		550
Delivery and transport	35	55	35		125
Administration					
Head office costs				85	85
Charged to divisions	25	38	22	(85)	
Total costs	235	323	202	–	760
Contribution	65	127	63	–	255

Figure 3.2 Another Company: building a 'complete picture'

In this instance the profit centres are obliged to bear a share of administration costs allocated in proportion to turnover.

4. Who provides the figures?

Like computers, budgets are only as good as the information put into them.

Allow somebody in head office to dream up figures and the result will be no better than a guess. Start by allowing the most senior managers to say what results they want, and again the budgets will be nothing more than aspirations which may be no nearer the truth.

Worse still, nobody will be committed to achieving the figures so neatly presented, nobody will feel responsible.

Budgeting should start at the lowest level practical. Anybody given responsibility for achieving, or keeping within, a budget should play a part in its setting.

It is those 'on the ground' who are best informed about their own tasks and who are most likely to come up with realistic figures. And once they have done so, they are committed to stand by them. This does not mean that anybody should be given a free hand in setting budgets. Far from it.

First, there need to be some ground rules. And then there needs to be a process of review and revision.

Ground rules

Budgets should be a realistic assessment of the probable. They should not be targets which might possibly be achieved given a following wind and a stroke or two of good luck.

Nor should they be figures that can be achieved easily, without effort or thought.

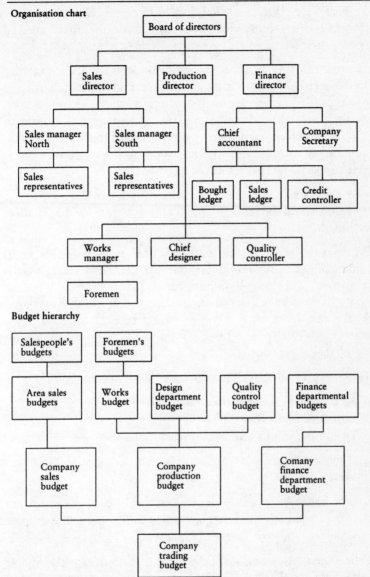

The budgeting hierarchy is a mirror image of the organisation chart. Budgeting starts at the lowest level of authority with 'cost centre' figures funnelled down to produce a company 'profit centre' overall trading budget. In a bigger company with a number of 'profit centres' each would have a similar budgeting hierarchy with the individual centres consolidated to produce a group budget.

Figure 4.1 *Yet Another Company: organisational and budgeting structure*

Targets have their uses when linked to commissions and other rewards. They are an aid to achieving results rather than expected results themselves.

The first rule given to those compiling budgets should be that they are responsible for meeting their budgets and will be regarded as having failed just as seriously if they fall under or romp over. Budgets are, after all, part of planning and control, an aid to making sure that the business moves forward in an orderly fashion, and is not diverted from its overall policy objectives and is able to use its limited resources to best effect.

The second rule is that the person setting his or her part of the budget should be able to justify and argue for the figures included.

Previous period results are inevitably used as the yardstick when setting budgets. But a thinking approach should be encouraged – what some call 'zero base budgeting'. In the extreme it means going back to basics, assuming nothing, questioning everything. At the very least, budget setters should be encouraged to open their minds to all possibilities, not simply to up last year's figures by whatever per cent.

Third, everybody has to use the same set of assumptions.

If the sales team assumes that inflation will be 5 per cent next year but the production people set their budgets based on 10 per cent inflation, the results will be distorted.

And what will be the level of wage increases next year; what will interest rates be?

A view has to be taken on all those factors outside the control of the business which will affect its trading. It is better that that view is consistent throughout the company.

True, it may then be consistently wrong, but at least the figures can be amended and updated more easily.

5. Profits are not the only measure

Management accounts that show how a business is faring from month to month usually concentrate on trading results. They net off income and expenditure figures down to a 'bottom line' to show a contribution or profit.

Likewise the attention in budgeting is directed first to income and expenditure measured on a similar basis to financial and management accounts.

But just as in financial accounts, a budget showing results alone – the anticipated profit and loss account – is not enough to give a rounded view of operations. There are two additional elements that are needed – 'capital' movements and cash flow.

Reporting convention

The almost universally accepted structure for the financial accounts of commercial enterprises comprises a trading statement showing profits and losses, a balance sheet showing financial structure and position, plus a funds flow statement showing cash movements.

Behind this reporting triumvirate lies accounting convention – the rules that accountants follow in building up a picture in numbers.

Accounting convention demands that some items of expenditure are treated as 'capital' items, some as 'revenue'.

The latter, like purchases and sales, are to do with day-to-day trading – things that are bought to be *used up*, rather than *used*

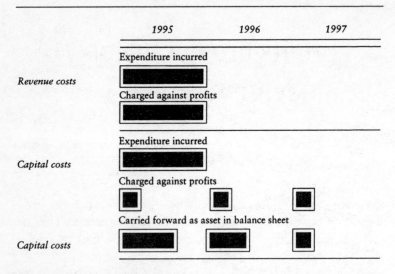

Capital expenditure is that made to acquire assets to use to generate income for the business over a number of years. Above, revenue expenditure is charged against profits in the year incurred. Capital expenditure has been written off over four years with a diminishing balance carried forward in the balance sheet. A budget that dealt with revenue only would therefore not show the whole story.

Figure 5.1 *Capital and revenue expenditure*

in the business, and sold to make an immediate return rather than to realise cash tied up in capital equipment.

The former are to do with the longer term and include, for example, purchases of premises, vehicles or plant.

If a van is purchased to be used in the business to earn profits over four years, it would be unfair to charge the whole cost against the year in which it is bought. So in calculating performance the cost is spread over the four-year working life of the van by way of an annual 'depreciation' equal to a quarter of the purchase price.

In the meantime the part of the cost of the van that has so far not been written off is a balance in the books, carried forward in the 'balance sheet' as an asset.

This means that revenue budgets do not show total expenditure

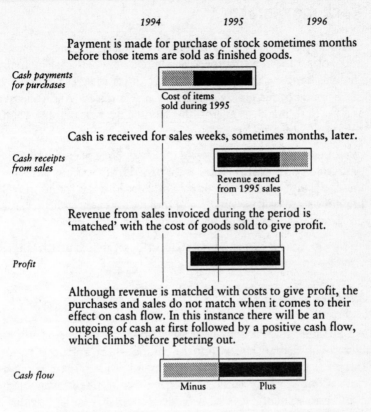

1994   *1995*   *1996*

Payment is made for purchase of stock sometimes months before those items are sold as finished goods.

Cash payments for purchases

Cost of items sold during 1995

Cash is received for sales weeks, sometimes months, later.

Cash receipts from sales

Revenue earned from 1995 sales

Revenue from sales invoiced during the period is 'matched' with the cost of goods sold to give profit.

Profit

Although revenue is matched with costs to give profit, the purchases and sales do not match when it comes to their effect on cash flow. In this instance there will be an outgoing of cash at first followed by a positive cash flow, which climbs before petering out.

Cash flow

Minus   Plus

So the 'matched' sales and purchases do not match at all when it comes to their effect on the bank statement.

Figure 5.2 *The matching concept and cash flow*

in a year, nor do they show how the business is or is not investing for the future.

And even if they did show both capital and revenue income and expenditure, accounting convention would ensure that these totals would still bear little more than passing similarity to the actual cash sums coming into and going out of the business.

Cash movements

Business performance is measured in terms of income achieved and costs incurred, irrespective almost of when cash actually changes hands. The business takes credit for its sales when delivery is made of the goods and an invoice is raised. And to arrive at a profit it 'matches' against this income the cost of those goods sold (see Figure 5.2).

Of course, the actual goods sold may well have been bought and paid for a good while before, even turned from various parts and materials into a finished product and kept in stock for months. If the goods are sold on credit, the money for them will probably not come in for at least a few weeks, perhaps longer.

So the 'matched' sales and purchases do not match at all when it comes to their effect on the bank statement.

Three views

All business transactions have cash flow consequences. Not all have an immediate effect upon the balance sheet, and not all upon the profits statement. On the other hand, a list of cash transactions alone – which would not distinguish between revenue and capital movements or acknowledge amounts owed and owing – would give no more indication of the wealth and prospects of the business than the personal bank balance of an individual. Are there large bills to pay? Does the person own a house or investments? Bank statements alone do not give the answer. All three views, showing the effects of transactions on profits (revenue), balance sheet (capital) and cash flow are needed to show how the business is doing.

Since budgeting is about planning and control, knowing what is possible and what is beyond present resources, and since profit statements alone do not show the whole picture, it is essential that budgets are prepared covering both capital spending plans and the expected cash consequences of trading.

Payment and receipts may not have direct impact on current trading results either because they result from or apply to the activities of another period or because they are 'capital' rather than 'revenue' in nature and impact mainly on the balance sheet.

	Revenue items	Capital items	Profit affected	Balance sheet affected	Cash flow affected
Sales income	Yes	No	Yes	Debtors from credit sales	Yes, but timing difference
Purchases of raw materials	Yes	No	Yes	Creditors from credit purchases	Yes, but timing difference
Purchases of goods for resale	Yes	No	Yes	Creditors credit purchases	Yes, but timing difference
Wages	Yes	No	Yes	PAYE element will be creditor	Yes
Overheads (excluding depreciation)	Yes	No	Yes	If paid in advance or arrears	Yes, but possible timing difference
Depreciation	Yes*	No	Yes	Yes	No
Borrowing	No, but interest is	Yes	No	Yes	Yes
Sale of fixed assets	No	Yes	Profit or loss on sale	Yes	Yes
Loan repayments	No	Yes	No	Yes	Yes
Purchase of fixed assets	No	Yes	Depreciation only	Yes	Yes

*Depreciation is a special case. It is a notional charge against profits calculated as a proportion of the cost of fixed assets in use with reference to their expected useful life. Cash flow is affected by the purchase of fixed assets but not by the depreciation charge.

Figure 5.3 *Revenue, capital and cash flow*

Capital ideas

Capital spending is an area that does not have such a direct link to sales. Surely new plant and equipment will make new processes possible, products cheaper or quicker, or both, to produce or deliver?

But there is usually a time delay. Sales for the coming year are not absolutely dependent on a new piece of equipment becoming available at a precise date. There is some leeway.

In businesses of any size capital projects, from building a new factory to replacing delivery vans, will be proposed, costed, shown to be viable and authorised well in advance.

Capital expenditure budgets will therefore tend to be lists of previously authorised projects showing the amounts involved and the timing of payments.

Also included will be expected projects yet to be approved and, usually, some discretionary or contingency amount for each manager.

Capital items are not necessarily bought in from outside. For example, staff could be used to build a new workshop or effect a major installation. If so, they should still be budgeted for in the same way, otherwise there will be a distorted view of costs and hence profitability.

How capital budgets are presented is again a matter of style and choice. Details that could be useful include a description of the capital project, reference back to the original proposal, details of when and by whom the project was authorised, and when it is expected to materialise. Timing of cash payments would also be helpful as the cash consequences of the capital expenditure must be written into the cash flow statements.

There are various investment appraisal techniques that can be used to assess the viability of individual capital projects. These include, for example, calculating the pay-back period, return on capital or the net present value.

The first method gives an indication of the risks involved since it is a simple measure of how long it will take the new piece of plant equipment or whatever to pay for itself in increased profits. A long pay-back period means that the risk is higher since the business is exposed to possible interest rate hikes or to increased competition, technical innovation or changes in the market it is serving.

Return on investment involves calculating the average profit (or saving) likely to result from using the new equipment and expressing this as a percentage of the cost. If the percentage is higher than the average interest rates the business is likely to pay and/or reaches predetermined targets, by this criterion it is worthwhile.

The more sophisticated methods of investment appraisal are based on what is known as the 'discounted cash flow' or 'net present value' method – the principle is the same in both, only the method of presenting the result differs.

As the name implies, this is concerned with the amount and timing of cash flows resulting from an investment rather than 'profit' or 'returns'. It is based on the notion that money in the hand today is worth more than money in the hand next year – the difference is the amount that could be earned by use of that money in the intervening period.

So all cash flows are discounted back to a present value to arrive at a net positive – or negative – total inflow or outflow expected for the investment.

These methods help to assess and control the risks of each individual project. But no matter what the size of the potential return, what these methods do not do is show whether resources are available to make the investment. Building capital projects into an overall plan by way of a budget shows what is possible, and what is most beneficial to the business as a whole.

Department	Nature of project		Authorisation		Expenditure payment		When in operation
		Ref	Date	Amount	Date	Amount	
Sales	Replace part car fleet	CA23	6/6/94	£38,000	1/3/95	£9,000	1/3/93
					1/6/95	£3,000	
					1/9/95	£3,000	
					1/12/95	£3,000	
					1996	£20,000	

Notes: This project was authorised at the main board meeting on 6 June last when it was agreed to replace seven of the car fleet used by the sales team. The cars being replaced, for which a trade-in value of £18,000 has been agreed, are now all over three years old with excess of 60,000 miles on the clock. The proposal CA23 put to the board showed a potential net return of £3,000 a year, mainly resulting from an expected saving in maintenance costs. The cars will be purchased using a hire purchase facility spread over two years. The interest rate quoted equates to 12 per cent per annum. Writing off the total cost of the vehicles – £38,000 plus £18,000 = £56,000 – over four years the depreciation charge will be £1,166 per month, commencing from the start of March. This compares with the current £875 per month depreciation charge for the vehicles being traded in.

The seven vehicles being sold have a book value of £10,500 – cost of £42,000 less three years' depreciation equal to £31,500.

Department	Nature of project		Authorisation		Expenditure payment		When in operation
Sales	Replace part car fleet	–	–	£38,000	1/9/95	£9,000	1/9/95
					1/12/95	£3,000	

Note: This project – for replacement of a further seven cars – has yet to be approved, although it will be required if our normal replacement pattern for sales staff's vehicles is to be maintained.

Department	Nature of project		Authorisation		Expenditure payment		When in operation
Works	Automatic lathe	CA45	7/9/94	£107,000	1994	£10,000	
					16/95	£50,000	
					1/8/95	£47,000	1/9/95

Notes: This project was authorised at the board meeting of 7 September. An order has already been placed for the lathe with the German manufacturers and a 10 per cent deposit paid. Delivery is promised for 1 June.

Some £7,000 of the cost relates to building alterations to accommodate the lathe and installation. This work will be completed by our own staff.

The lathe, which will increase capacity in the turning area by 35 per cent, has been purchased in anticipation of an increase in pump sales towards the end of next year. It is expected to be operational by 1 September.

The investment appraisal submitted with the proposal showed a pay-back of two years and average return on investment of 23 per cent.

Department	Nature of project		Authorisation		Expenditure payment		When in operation
Accounts	Office furniture	CA32	10/10/94	£5,000	1/2/95	£5,000	4/1/95

Notes: This project was authorised by the finance director who has discretion to authorise capital projects up to £5,000. The furniture has already been ordered and will be delivered in early January.

Figure 5.4 *Madeup Engineering Company: capital budgets*

Preparing a cash flow statement

One of the most important limitations on what is possible is cash availability.

The cash flow statement is similar to other budget statements but records not a weekly, monthly or quarterly estimate of revenue earned or the 'matched' costs – the figures that would appear in the profit and loss account – but the expected receipts and payments, including those associated with 'capital' items. The object is to arrive at an estimate of the bank balance likely at the end of each budgeting interval.

This means that any Value Added Tax on sales or purchases must be added to the net-of-VAT figures included in the budget. It also means delaying sales revenues by the average time customers take to pay invoices and adjusting the timing of raw material costs to take account of manufacturing periods, changes in stock levels and supplier credit terms. And depreciation charges must be excluded – depreciation is not an actual cash payment.

A fuller explanation of cash flow budgeting is included in *Cash Flow and How to Improve It*, another title in this 'Business Basics' series.

Just as compiling budgets is usually a matter of working from the particular to the general, a careful step-by-step process, so putting together a cash flow statement involves calculations using the same basic information. The degree of detail included and the interval frequency used will depend very much upon the size and nature of the business and possibly on the tightness of the margins within which it has to work.

While it would be pointless to produce statements in more detail than needed for accuracy and understanding, the actual calculations themselves need not be unduly cumbersome given access to a personal computer and spreadsheet program, which make the whole process relatively painless.

		Jan £	Feb £	Mar £	Total £
Receipts	Trading – Sales	36,542	43,592	46,176	126,310
	Capital – Sale of land			25,000	25,000
Total		36,542	43,592	71,176	151,310
Payments:	Manufacturing costs – Raw materials – Casings	5,875	12,455	5,287	23,617
	Rods	1,125	1,845	1,650	4,620
	Wages (excluding PAYE)	4,900	8,600	5,100	18,600
	PAYE	2,000	2,700	4,200	8,900
	Overheads (excluding depreciation and rent)	2,000	1,750	2,500	6,250
	Rent		5,000		5,000
	Sales and marketing costs	2,500	3,600	3,600	9,700
	Distribution costs	3,300	3,750	4,500	11,550
	Administration costs	3,000	3,000	3,000	9,000
	Finance costs Hire purchase interest	900	900	900	2,700
	Bank interest		600		600
	Other – Taxation	17,000			17,000
	VAT		9,600		9,600
	New car (deposit)	5,000			5,000
	Hire purchase repayments	3,000	3,000	3,000	9,000
Total		50,600	56,800	33,737	141,137
Net movement		−14,058	−13,208	37,439	10,173
Opening bank balance		19,600	5,542	−7,666	19,600
Net movement		−14,058	−13,208	37,439	10,173
Closing bank balance		5,542	−7,666	29,773	29,773

Figure 5.5 *Madeup Engineering Company: summary cash flow statement – first quarter 1993*

Standard trade terms for pump casings are 30 days' credit. In practice 60 per cent of customers pay on time while the remainder hold out for 60 days. The company has secured a major contract for the supply of 15,000 casings in February. Negotiations were tough and Madeup was knocked down to a price of just 80p per casing. However, the customer agreed to pay 50 per cent of the invoice cash on delivery with the remainder 30 days later.

Piston rods are sold to one major customer only with payment of each invoice made on 60 days.

Regular deliveries of both products are made throughout every month so that an average mid-month invoicing date is assumed for the purposes of estimating cash flow.

Expected receipts *Pump casings:*	Total £	Jan £	Feb £	Mar £
November 1992 sales £21,000 plus VAT	24,675	9,870	–	–
December 1992 sales £16,500 plus VAT	19,387	11,632	7,754	–
January 1993 sales £22,500 plus VAT	26,437	–	15,863	10,574
February 1993 sales £18,000 plus VAT	21,150	–	–	12,690
February 1993 special contract £12,000 plus VAT	14,100	–	7,050	7,050
March 1993 sales £23,940 plus VAT	28,130	–	–	–
Piston rods: November 1992 sales £12,800 plus VAT	15,040	15,040	–	–
December 1992 sales £11,000 plus VAT	12,925	–	12,925	–
January 1993 sales £13,500 plus VAT	15,862	–	–	15,862
February 1993 sales £12,000 plus VAT	14,100	–	–	–
March 1993 sales £15,200 plus VAT	17,860	–	–	–
Total cash receipts		36,542	43,592	46,176

Figure 5.6 *Madeup Engineering Company: sales receipts – cash flow calculation – (first quarter 1993)*

Sales income

For example, filling in the anticipated bankings resulting from sales is a matter of adjusting back for the delay between issuing an invoice and actually receiving a cheque in payment and adding on the Value Added Tax.

Provided sales are not dominated by one or just a few large customers and that payment experience does not vary dramatically between different classes of customer, it will usually be quite adequate to use averages to make these adjustments.

Where there are substantial differences in agreed or accepted trade terms between different classes of customer, separate cash flow calculations may have to be made for each class.

6. Where management comes in

Given that budgeted figures well up from the base of the organisational pyramid, it might seem that senior managers have a limited role to play in the process. Not so.

Producing annual budgets is a multi-staged affair.

First, the budgeting structure has to be decided, parameters drawn, and figures collected and collated.

A first draft of the budget is drawn up. And then the debate begins. The results will not be as good as expected, somebody will be unhappy that their budget has been cut, somebody else that a capital project has been put off.

Management has a part to play at each stage.

Budgeting structure

Although budgeting should start at the lowest level, this does not mean that everybody should have a budget.

Sometimes, and sometimes by default, it is left to the finance department to collect figures from whichever people it thinks fit. But this is to ignore the influence which budget setting and keeping has on those involved. Budgeting is more than just an information-gathering exercise.

As said earlier, budgets impose responsibility. Deciding who and at what level budgets should be set is something which has considerable bearing on how a business is run.

It is therefore a management decision worth considering at a high level.

The general ambience in which budgeting and budgetary control operates is another area of management concern.

It should be clear to all that the object of the exercise is not to pummel figures into a financial model that looks acceptable if this bears little relationship to reality.

Massaging the figures

Once set, budgets are not there to be manipulated.

In cost centres there is always a tendency for managers to make sure that their total budget is spent by the end of the year, for fear that otherwise next year's budget will be cut.

Here, perhaps, is where the power of zero base budgeting – or at least the underlying idea – should be brought to bear. And this should be at all levels of management so that it is understood senior managers will agree budgets based on what they expect to happen next year rather than what happened last year.

Nor should manipulating expenditure between different budget allocations be made an acceptable way of doing things.

Sometimes managers, seeing that they have underspent on, say, their repairs and maintenance budget but have used up their capital expenditure budget, will try to sneak through capital expenditure under the guise of a repair.

Harmless? Not really. Such massaging of the figures means nobody really knows the overall picture of spending, decisions are distorted and next year's budgets are set on a false premise.

Senior management can set the tone by the way in which it approaches the budgeting process and the importance it gives to it.

Another Service Company:
Budget preparation sheet – salary costs

Location:..		Budget preparation sheet CC1		
Department:...		Year end...................................		
Manager:..		Date prepared...........................		

Current staff:	Name	Role number	Current salary £	Budgeted cost £
	....	....	....	
	....	....	....	
	....	....	....	
	....	....	....	

Additional staff: Expected joining date			Expected salary £	
	....		....	
	....		....	
	....		....	

Total

Total last year

Budgeted last year

	Last year	Budgeted for
Average number of staff: (Treat each employee not with the department for the full year as 1/12 × the number of full months worked)		

1. We are expecting to award pay increases averaging 3 per cent next March. For the purposes of budgeting, you should assume that the current salary of each person will apply for the first three months of the year, and the current salary plus 3 per cent for the next nine months. Budgeted salary costs should be the total salary for the year plus 14 per cent to account for employer's National Insurance and pension and sick pay provisions.
2. Explain below the reasons for any increase or decrease in budgeted staff numbers, the tasks they will perform and reasons why the expected salary should be higher or lower than staff currently employed to perform similar duties. Explain also reasons for significant differences in the salary costs budgeted or incurred last year and those budgeted for next year.

Figure 6.1a *Another Service Company: cost centre budget pro-forma – salary costs*

Another Service Company:
Budget preparation sheet – consumables

Location:................................   Budget preparation sheet CC2

Department:............................   Year end................................

Manager:................................   Date prepared...............

Nature of consumables	Last year		Next year
	Actual £	Budget £	Budget £
....			
....			
....			
....			
....			
....			
Total			

1. We are estimating an average inflation rate of 3.5 per cent next year and this increase should be applied to current prices when budgeting for next year. Where we have fixed price contracts – as in the case of print supplies, for example – assume that a 3.5 per cent price increase will apply from the date that the present contract ends.
2. Explain below reasons for budgeted increases or decreases other than those related to expected price increases related to inflation. Expected significant changes in quantities used or price expected changes more or less than 3.5 per cent should be detailed.

Figure 6.1b *(continued)* Another Service Company: cost centre budget pro-forma – consumables

Another Service Company:
Budget preparation sheet – Profit centre trading

Location:................................ Budget preparation sheet PC1

Division:............................... Year end...............................

Manager:............................... Date prepared.......................

| | Last year | | Next year |
	Actual £	Budget £	Budget £
Income: (from form R1)			
Marketing department			
Salaries (from form CC1)			
Advertising (from form CC3)			
Consumables (from form CC2)			
Staff expenses (from form CC4)			
Total			
Customer service department			
Salaries (from form CC1)			
Consumables (from form CC2)			
Staff expenses (from form CC4)			
Total			
Administration department			
Salaries (from form CC1)			
Consumables (from form CC2)			
Staff expenses (from form CC4)			
Accommodation costs (from form CC5)			
Total			
Total costs			
Contribution			

Profit centre budgets of this type are constructed by consolidating a
number of cost centre budgets compiled using standard forms. So, in the
example above, marketing, customer service and administration departmental managers would each have completed a salary cost pro-forma
budget sheet.

Figure 6.1c *Another Service Company – Profit centre budget
pro-forma*

The same set of rules

In all but the least complicated of businesses, budget setting is best done by way of a coordinated set of paperwork, pro-forma sheets issued to those selected for budget setting and keeping responsibility.

The advantage is that everybody involved tackles the problem in the same way. For example, the analysis of costs will be uniform, allowing comparisons to be made with former years and across departments.

Also, the forms can include notes on preparation and key assumptions, such as the rate of inflation or expected wage increases.

And space can be left to explain significant changes from last year so that there is information available when it comes to checking budgets for consistency of logic and arithmetic accuracy and reviewing and revising the figures.

Just like budgets themselves, there is no 'right' way to produce this paperwork. It is a matter of individual tailoring to fit the chosen managerial structure of the firm and its chosen line of business and to meet the needs of the day.

7. Uncertainties and assumptions

Senior managers also have an important part to play in dealing with uncertainties and assumptions.

Every business faces uncertainties. After all, one definition of the entrepreneurial role is that of 'risk taking'. If there were no uncertainties there would be no risks.

But it is those uncertainties that are not recognised and assessed – like the rock lurking beneath the surface in wait for the unsuspecting tanker – that are the most likely to become dangers.

The starting point for dealing with the problem is therefore to identify the most important uncertainties, and to differentiate between those which arise from decisions of the business and those over which it has no influence. Examples of the first might be the effect of raising prices by 10 per cent or of launching a new product. Examples of the second include the rate of inflation or the level of interest rates.

Uncertainties arising from management decisions can be assessed individually and monitored. If they veer towards the unfavourable, the decision can be reversed or amended or other action taken to avert disaster.

It is only when a decision on a known and likely project remains pending at budget time that there is a budgeting problem. Otherwise, the business will be set on a particular course and will have already assessed the most likely outcome.

But somebody has to take a view on how pending decisions and those uncertainties outside the control of the business will affect budgets.

Reasonable or wrong

Estimations of outcome can only be proved reasonable or wrong after the event. Even so, they should be approached in a logical way that is capable of scrutiny and amendment, and those estimations should be applied consistently throughout. That way it will be obvious when assumptions no longer hold good and relatively easy to recalculate figures using revised assumptions.

Budgets cannot deal with every eventuality. Dealing with the prospect of a world war would not be a productive exercise for the foreseeable future. But for a company that exports bullet-proof vests the likelihood of an uprising in a developing market might well enter its thinking.

Each business will have its own list of significant uncertainties on which some features will be common, some unique. It is a list that those responsible for suggesting budget numbers should have to hand and apply.

Risky business

Putting a number to an uncertainty is not the end of the story. Numbers look safe and precise. But they are not. They hide the risks involved.

If the rock beneath the surface is large enough to sink the ship it is good seamanship to work to the outer limits of navigating accuracy. So if a fix is accurate to within 500 yards, a course should be steered that takes the vessel a safe distance from the danger, plus 500 yards.

The same principle applies in business. A course needs to be plotted away from the dangers. But first you have to know where the rocks lie.

Budgets themselves will reveal some of the dangers – running out of cash in August, not having enough production capacity to meet

To managers with budgeting responsibility
When compiling your budgets for next year you should build in the following assumptions:

Overall
Inflation: We are assuming that inflation will average 5 per cent next year. Except where listed below, this figure should be built into all cost and revenue figures.

Market conditions: We are predicting that consumer spending will increase by 10 per cent next year which suggests a 5 per cent increase in real terms.

Exchange rates: Assume that exchange rates with all our major supplier countries will remain unchanged next year.

Interest: We are estimating that interest rates will remain at 7 per cent next year but will rise to an average of 9 per cent the following year.

Wages: The autumn Budget included an increase of 10 per cent in National Insurance costs from next April. We do not predict further increases during the year.

Except for production costs, an average wage increase of 5 per cent should be assumed for budgeting purposes.

Production costs
Wages: The GGDDU has submitted an industry claim for a 12 per cent wage increase. Negotiations are continuing but budgets should be prepared on the basis of an 8 per cent settlement together with a productivity commitment that should enable us to increase output per hour by 4 per cent.

Materials: Our cereal requirements have been bought forward until June after which we expect prices to increase by 3 per cent.

Packaging: Environmental laws will require a change to a more expensive packaging material. Assume a 20 per cent increase in packaging material for production after 1 July.

Despatch
Fuel costs: Assume an 8 per cent increase in fuel costs plus an additional 2 per cent from November when we expect excise duties to be raised.

Road tax: Assume an additional £30 per vehicle from 1 November.

Sales: Prices of our leading brands will be increased by 3 per cent on 1 March and a further 3 per cent on 1 November.

Madeup Luxury Foods has decided that the above assumptions are key to its budget setting and has circulated this sheet to all those with responsibility for producing budgets.

Figure 7.1 *Madeup Luxury Foods: budget assumptions*

sales, losing money because overheads are running out of control, and so on.

But other dangers, those resulting from major uncertainties, remain masked by the comforting figures worked up from assumptions.

Enter sensitivity analysis.

The possible and the probable

The idea of budgeting is to show the most likely outcome of trading. But the most likely outcome is not the only outcome. It is probably probable, given a reasonable approach, that budgets can get somewhere near the mark most of the time.

It is almost certain that they will be wide of the mark sometimes.

Some elements of the budget – say, the assessment of sales, or of the time it takes to install a new piece of equipment – will be more influential in promoting a wayward assessment than others. It may be that the element itself is volatile, but not necessarily so. The cause of the problem will be the 'knock-on' effect on different parts of the business.

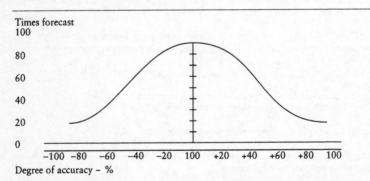

A typical probability curve showing how, in this example, actual results turned out in most cases to be within 20 per cent of budgeted figure, less frequently out by plus or minus up to 60 per cent and very occasionally by up to 80 per cent. If budgeting has any degree of accuracy it will produce a similar probability curve.

Figure 7.2 *The law of averages at work*

Bringing a new piece of plant into production three months late will mean additional unplanned overtime and an increase in bought-in parts and sub-contracting to meet orders. Costs will exceed sales prices and profits will tumble. Quality control will suffer and goods will be returned. Invoices will remain unpaid while errors are put right and cash flow will dry up.

The rock does not have to be large to cause damage, just hard and sharp and at the right depth.

Sensitivity analysis is a jargon term for a search for these rogue business rocks.

Best, worst and likely

Generally, budgeters are interested in three possible results: the best possible, the worst possible and the most likely. Estimates of the most likely outcome of trading provide the most useful budgets. Estimates of best and worst results reveal the degree of risk involved.

There are a number of ways to get to the, usually theoretical, extremes, which can be used both in individual investment appraisals and in assessment of budget risks as a whole. They each involve a similar degree of assessment to the original budgeting process, so are themselves no more than best estimates subject to a similar degree of uncertainty.

Range of results

One approach is to treat each assumption, indeed even each line of the budget, not as one probable outcome but as a possible range. Each line therefore has a best possible, a worst and a most likely result.

The budget can then be calculated three times showing the likely and the highly unlikely but theoretically possible.

While this may give an idea of the parameters and suggest the figures liable to the widest fluctuation, it does little to pinpoint which are most significant in terms of overall result.

Cost: New automatic lathe			£175,000
Less: resale value of old lathe £50,000 (70% probability)			35,000
Net cost			£140,000

Savings	Estimate (£000)	Probability factor (%)	Probable outcome (£)
Wages			
First year	10	50	5,000
Second year	40	75	30,000
Third year	40	85	34,000
Fourth year	40	90	36,000
Fifth year	40	95	38,000
Total	170		143,000
Materials			
First year	4	50	2,000
Second year	12	80	9,600
Third year	12	85	10,200
Fourth year	12	85	10,200
Fifth year	12	85	10,200
Total	52		42,200
Total savings	222		185,200
Additional costs:			
Depreciation at 20 per cent per annum			140,000
Net saving			£45,200
Average saving per annum			£9,040
Return on capital 9,040 × 100 ÷ 140,000 =			6.4%

Another Madeup Company is considering purchasing a new automatic lathe with an estimated life of five years. The cost is £175,000 but the lathe it replaces can be sold for its book value of £35,000, bringing the net cost down to £140,000. At first glance the purchase seems a winner. With anticipated net savings of £82,000 (£222,000 – £140,000) over five years, or an average of £16,400 per annum, the return on investment would be 11.7 per cent (£16,400 × 100 ÷ 140,000). But all this is conjecture. The timing of the installation and the period needed to train operators up to strength are critical to achieving the anticipated savings. Once probability factors have been applied, the percentage return, at 6.4 per cent, works out to less than the interest charge on the funds which the business would need to borrow to finance the deal.

Figure 7.3 *Probability in action: Another Madeup Company – purchase of new lathe*

Another idea is to attach a probability factor to each figure. This approach can be used in investment appraisal in a similar way to the discounted cash flow appraisal method. But in this case figures are discounted, not according to the timing of cash flows but according to their probability.

What if?

Once, budgeting preparation was a laborious task. Figures had to be collated, calculations made, columns created and additions made down and across. There was a limit to the amount of work that could reasonably be done to look at different possibilities. That is no longer true.

The accounting department of virtually every business of any size has access to computers. Accounting software has made invoicing, payroll, VAT calculations, management and financial reporting much easier. And spreadsheet packages have come to the aid of the budget preparers.

These packages allow businesses to create a template for their budgets in which calculations, additions and subtractions become an automatic function. All that needs to be entered are the base figures and assumptions.

This means that it is no great chore, or at least not as great a chore as it used to be, to recalculate budgets once, twice, or many more times using different key assumptions.

What if interest rates next year were not 7 per cent but 12 per cent? What if the value of the pound fell sharply against the US dollar? What if competition caused us to cut our prices by 12 per cent? What if average pay rises were 7 per cent rather than 3 per cent? And so it goes on.

Budgets can be recalculated for each possibility, revealing whether or not the consequences are desirable, problematical or terminal.

Flexible budgeting

This technique – 'what if analysis' – can be carried forward into the trading year. Then 'what if?' becomes 'what was'.

Known as 'flexible budgeting', the idea is that budgets are constantly updated to take account of what has happened in the year so far.

There are arguments for and against doing this. Moving the goal posts may not gain the same staff commitment that a more definite plan will achieve. And then there is the work involved. Businesses make money by making and selling things, by actually doing rather than saying what they have done or will do. Budgeting is a management aid and resources put towards these activities should not outweigh the benefits.

Against this, it is clearly ridiculous, and probably dangerous, to continue to work on the basis of a budget which has been obviously overtaken by events. In an extreme example, if the factory burns down what use is the budget then? Perhaps closer to home, what about when sales are significantly less than budgeted? Should recruitment plans be carried through, planned purchases of new plant and equipment go ahead?

For most businesses the best solution probably lies in the middle course. There is a budget for the year which is kept under review and updated, say, six monthly or to take account of major events which make the original budget invalid.

8. An example

No two businesses are identical. They vary according to the markets they serve, the resources available, management philosophy, and in a host of other ways.

It follows that if management accounts are to fit in with the objectives and aspirations of each business, and show up those aspects considered the most important, their structure cannot follow a standard form. Effective use of budgeting means applying general principles to particular situations.

Below is an example of how one imaginary business might budget.

The background

Madeup Turner Trading is a small engineering firm that produces two product lines, Nuts & bolts, and Screws. Until now over half its output has been sold directly to a large do-it-yourself chain. The rest it sells on contract to motor manufacturers. That proportion is about to change with the winning of a major new contract with a motor industry client. From the start of the second quarter this contract will increase turnover by over a quarter.

The business has only one factory and a small salesforce, with one salesperson for each of four geographical areas and one covering the motor industry. To meet the new contract it will have to buy two new lathes to add to the five that it already operates.

For the purposes of budgeting there are three cost centres: sales, production and administration.

Product – Nuts & bolts

Area	First qtr Units (000)	Value (£)	Second qtr Units (000)	Value (£)	Third qtr Units (000)	Value (£)	Fourth qtr Units (000)	Value (£)	Year Units (000)	Value (£)
East	440	22,000	600	30,000	660	33,000	440	22,000	2,140	107,000
Price		5p		5p		5p		5p		5p
North	600	30,000	1,200	48,000	1,200	48,000	800	40,000	3,800	166,000
Price		5p		4p		4p		5p		4.4p
South	500	25,000	700	35,000	900	45,000	500	25,000	2,600	130,000
Price		5p		5p		5p		5p		5p
West	300	15,000	1,000	50,000	1,000	50,000	800	40,000	3,100	155,000
Price		5p		5p		5p		5p		5p
Auto	2,000	60,000	3,000	90,000	2,000	60,000	3,300	99,000	10,300	309,000
Price		3p		3p		3p		3p		3p
(new)					3,800	95,000	3,800	95,000	7,600	190,000
Price						2.5p		2.5p		2.5p
Total	3,840	152,000	6,500	253,000	9,560	331,000	9,640	321,000	29,540	1057,000
Ave. price		4p		3.9p		3.5p		3.3p		3.6p
Last year	3,680	140,000	5,900	224,000	5,750	230,000	5,025	201,000	20,355	795,000
		3.8p		3.8p		4.0p		4.0p		3.9p

Increase over last year:

Units	4.3%		10.2%		66.3%		91.8%		45.1%	
Price	5.3%		2.6%		(13.5%)		(17.5%)		(7.7%)	
Value	8.6%		12.9%		43.0%		59.7%		33.0%	

Product – Screws

Area	First qtr Units (000)	Value (£)	Second qtr Units (000)	Value (£)	Third qtr Units (000)	Value (£)	Fourth qtr Units (000)	Value (£)	Year Units (000)	Value (£)
East	200	4,000	150	4,500	150	4,500	170	5,100	660	18,100
Price		2p		3p		3p		3p		2.7p
North	80	1,600	70	2,100	80	2,400	100	3,000	330	9,100
Price		2p		3p		3p		3p		2.75p
South	100	2,000	80	2,400	80	2,400	80	2,400	340	9,200
Price		2p		3p		3p		3p		2.7p
West	70	1,400	30	900	50	1,500	60	1,800	210	5,600
Price		2p		3p		3p		3p		2.7p
Total	450	9,000	330	9,900	360	10,800	410	12,300	1,540	42,000
Ave. price		2p		3p		3p		3p		2.7p
Last year	450	9,000	450	9,000	500	10,000	450	9,000	1,850	37,000
		2p		2p		2p		2p		2p

Increase over last year:

Units	–		(26.6%)		(28%)		(8.9%)		(16.8%)	
Price	–		50%		50%		50%		35%	
Value	–		10%		8%		37%		14%	
Total	161,000		262,900		341,800		333,300		1099,000	
Last year	149,000		233,000		240,000		210,000		832,000	

Figure 8.1 *Madeup Turner Trading: total sales budget*

Scheduled production	Units (000)	Units (000)	Units (000)	Units (000)	Units (000)
Nuts & bolts	4,700	6,600	8,500	9,600	29,400
Screws	450	330	360	410	1,550

| Indirect costs | | | Quarters | | |
	First £	Second £	Third £	Fourth £	Year £
Depreciation	10,000	10,000	15,000	15,000	50,000
Repairs and maintenance	2,500	2,500	2,800	2,800	10,600
Heat, light and power	8,700	9,000	12,000	12,000	41,700
Indirect wages	7,000	7,000	7,000	7,000	28,000
Total	28,200	28,500	36,800	36,800	130,300
Allocated					
Nuts & bolts	22,560	22,800	31,540	31,540	108,440
Screws	5,640	5,700	5,260	5,260	21,860

Figure 8.2 *Madeup Turner Trading: production budget – indirect costs*

| | | | Quarters | | |
	First £	Second £	Third £	Fourth £	Year £
Materials	32,430	45,540	87,975	99,360	265,305
Wages	22,560	31,680	47,600	53,760	155,600
Total variable costs	54,990	77,220	135,575	153,120	420,905
Cost per unit	1.17p	1.17p	1.60p	1.60p	1.43p
Indirect costs	22,560	22,800	31,540	31,540	108,440
Total costs	77,550	100,020	167,115	184,660	529,345
Cost per unit	1.65	1.51	2.0	1.92	1.8

Nuts & Bolts

| Cost of sales and stock | | | | Quarters | | | | |
| | First | | Second | | Third | | Fourth | |
	Units (000)	Value £	Units (000)	Value £	Units (000)	Value £	Units (000)	Value £
Opening stock	1,200	19,800	2,060	33,990	2,160	33,425	1,100	20,545
Add production	4,700	77,550	6,600	100,020	8,500	167,115	9,600	184,660
Total	5,900	97,350	8,660	134,010	10,660	200,540	10,700	205,205
Less sales	3,840	63,360	6,500	100,585	9,560	179,995	9,640	184,875
Closing stock	2,060	33,990	2,160	33,425	1,100	20,545	1,060	20,330
Cost per unit		1.65		1.54		1.86		1.92

Figure 8.3 *Madeup Turner Trading: production budget – Nuts and bolts*

60 Budgeting for business

	First £	Second £	Third £	Fourth £	Year £
			Quarters		
Salaries	28,000	28,000	32,000	32,000	120,000
Expenses	6,000	9,000	8,000	7,000	30,000
Car depreciation	3,000	3,000	3,000	3,000	12,000
Advertising and promotional literature	2,000	28,000	5,000	10,000	45,000
Total	39,000	68,000	48,000	52,000	207,000
Last year	35,000	45,000	45,000	35,000	160,000
Percentage increase	11.4%	51.1%	6.7%	48.6%	29.4%

Figure 8.4 *Madeup Turner Trading: sales and marketing department costs*

	First £	Second £	Third £	Fourth £	Year £
			Quarters		
Salaries	44,000	44,000	49,000	49,000	186,000
Expenses	2,500	2,500	2,500	2,500	10,000
Postage, printing and stationery	6,000	6,000	6,000	6,000	24,000
Rent and rates	11,000	23,000	23,000	23,000	80,000
Car depreciation	2,000	2,000	3,000	3,000	10,000
Computer depreciation	2,000	2,000	6,000	6,000	16,000
Furniture depreciation	500	500	500	500	2,000
Total	68,000	80,000	90,000	90,000	328,000
Last year	66,000	68,000	69,000	66,000	269,000
Percentage increase	3.0%	17.6%	30.4%	36.4%	21.9%

Figure 8.5 *Madeup Turner Trading: administration department costs*

	First £	Second £	Third £	Fourth £	Year £
			Quarters		
New lathes	–	–	200,000	–	200,000
(Depreciation rate 10% per annum)					
Cars – Admin dept	–	–	16,000	–	16,000
(Depreciation rate 25% per annum)					
Computer equipment	–	–	64,000	–	64,000
(Depreciation rate 25% per annum)					
Total	–	–	280,000	–	280,000

Figure 8.6 *Madeup Turner Trading: capital expenditure budget*

	First £	Second £	Quarters Third £	Fourth £	Year £
Sales income					
Nuts & bolts	152,000	253,000	331,000	321,000	1057,000
Screws	9,000	9,900	10,800	12,300	42,000
Total	161,000	262,900	341,800	333,300	1099,000
Production costs					
Nuts & bolts	63,360	100,585	179,995	184,875	528,815
Screws	13,000	14,400	15,650	17,925	60,975
Total	76,360	114,985	195,645	202,800	589,790
Contribution					
Nuts & bolts	88,640	152,415	151,005	136,125	528,185
Screws	(4,000)	(4,500)	(4,850)	(5,625)	(18,975)
Total	84,640	147,915	146,155	130,500	509,210
Overheads					
Sales and marketing	39,000	68,000	48,000	52,000	207,000
Administration	68,000	80,000	90,000	90,000	328,000
Total overheads	107,000	148,000	138,000	142,000	535,000
Net contribution	(22,360)	(85)	8,155	(11,500)	(25,790)
Leasing			2,000	2,000	4,000
Finance charges			2,500	2,500	5,000
			4,500	4,500	9,000
Net profit	(22,630)	(85)	3,655	(16,000)	(34,790)
Last year	(21,400)	9,100	12,700	9,600	10,000

Figure 8.7 *Madeup Turner Trading: trading summary*

	First £	Second £	Third £	Fourth £	Year £
Receipts					
Sales	246,000	189,000	309,000	401,000	1145,000
Bank loan		150,000			150,000
Total	246,000	339,000	309,000	401,000	1295,000
Payments					
Production costs Fixed costs:					
Repairs and maintenance	2,900	2,900	2,900	3,300	12,000
Heat, light and power	10,200	10,200	10,500	12,100	43,000
Wages	7,000	7,000	7,000	7,000	28,000
Variable:					
Nuts & bolts	55,000	59,000	81,500	143,500	339,000
Screws	3,500	3,500	4,400	5,900	17,300
Sales & marketing	33,500	37,800	69,700	47,500	188,500
Administration	73,800	75,500	76,800	80,700	306,800
VAT	15,050	(7,850)	24,600	37,000	68,800
Capital expenditure:					
Lathes	58,750	176,250			235,000
Cars		4,000	1,500	1,500	7,000
Loan repayments			7,500	7,500	15,000
Leasing Computer equipment		8,000	2,000	2,000	12,000
Finance charges			2,500	2,500	5,000
Total	259,700	376,300	290,900	350,500	1277,400
Balance brought forward	83,000	69,300	32,000	50,100	83,000
Add receipts	246,000	339,000	309,000	401,000	1295,000
	329,000	408,300	341,000	451,100	1378,000
Less payments	259,700	376,300	290,900	350,500	1277,400
Balance carried forward	69,300	32,000	50,100	100,600	100,600

Figure 8.8 *Madeup Turner Trading: cash flow statement*

9. A logical approach

Budgeting and budgetary control are exercises in logic. Madeup Turner Trading applied logic to build up its budgets for next year, in the process overcoming many of the problems common to budgeting.

The company decided that, for its purposes, quarterly figures gave sufficient detail. In most real situations this would not be the case, especially when it comes to cash flow.

Each cash flow balance is a snapshot of a certain position. And like a film, cash flow statements only give the moving picture when a number of frames are shown in quick succession. Monthly figures are usually the minimum needed to do this.

The general message is that budgets should be detailed enough to serve their purpose usefully but only that detailed. Any more and the effort is wasted.

Sales figures

The sales figures are the cornerstone on which Madeup Turner Trading's budgets have been built.

Included in the budgets are both units and sales value, and hence a unit price.

Information of this sort not only helps in calculation and checking, but also provides insights that will become valuable at budget review time.

In the case of Madeuup Turner Trading's Nuts & bolts sales

budget they highlight, for example, the lower unit price achieved in the motor industry sales and the even lower price accepted under the new contract. A clear link is revealed between volume and price that might become vital in later discussions.

Likewise, the Screws sales budget shows that a planned increase in sales price will have a direct link to the number of units that are expected to be sold.

Production costs

Once the expected sales have been settled the production department can work out its level of output.

Notice that output does not necessarily equal sales in the shorter term. This is because stock provides a buffer.

Knowing that it has to meet the demands of the new motor industry contract and that new equipment may take time to reach full production, the company plans to build up stock in the first half of the year, letting it run down again towards the close.

To arrive at a cost of production the business calculates fixed costs and then allocates these between its two product lines in proportion to the number of lathes used for each. In the first half of the year there are five lathes in total, one of which is used to produce screws. In the second half of the year it is planned that the two new lathes should come into use. So while one-fifth of fixed costs are charged to Screws in the first two quarters, only one-seventh of the (increased) fixed costs are charged to this product line in the third and fourth quarters.

Madeup Turner Trading treats the heat, light and power costs of the factory as a fixed cost as a matter of expediency on the grounds that it does not meter each lathe. But where the cost is significant it would be better to install some way of measuring power costs and treating these as variable, which is patently the case.

Likewise, wage costs are treated as variable because the firm employs a number of part-time employees who can be called in at will. But should the workforce be less flexible and overtime or staffing up be required to meet different levels of production, a more sophisticated calculation might be called for.

The cost of sales is taken by averaging the cost of stock brought forward and of production during the quarter. So in the second quarter, for example, the opening stock of Nuts & bolts was 2,060,000 units with a brought-forward value of £33,990, or 1.65p per unit.

During the quarter a further 6,600,000 units were produced at a cost of £100,020, or 1.51p per unit. The total of both stock and production were 8,660,000 units at £134,010, or 1.54p per unit. And it is this weighted average price that has been used to value both the cost of sales and the stock carried forward.

Sales and marketing

The sales and marketing department costs are those estimated as necessary to achieve the budgeted sales. Salary costs are anticipated to rise mid-year as the result of planned pay increases. If a large commission element were involved in salespeople's salaries, there would also be an element of fluctuation in proportion to sales.

Advertising and promotional literature expenses show a marked increase with no immediate link to sales, the marketing manager arguing that this cost is in part an investment for the future and necessary to overcome the objections to the planned increases in the price of Screws.

Administration department

Administration costs are relatively fixed in nature, but here too a planned increase in salaries is reflected in the budgeted salary costs.

Rent and rates will also go up during the year, not a matter directly under the control of the business in the short term, although in the longer term it can always take the decision to move premises.

Car and computer depreciation charges are budgeted to increase during the year, reflecting the spending in this area written into the capital expenditure budget.

Trading summary

All these elements – sales, production and other costs, and capital expansion and replacement plans – are brought together in the trading summary.

This reveals that, while sales will be up by quite a margin, profits will disappear if the business continues on its current course. It might be prepared to take a loss for a year or two if this were the cost of gaining a stronger market position, although there is no sign of it here.

Clearly some re-thinking is called for.

Cash flow

But not all is lost.

The cash flow statement shows that, albeit with some additional borrowing, the cash position will remain viable.

The reason is that while sales revenue is generally postponed to reflect the credit allowed to customers, most costs – rent and rates, which are paid in advance, are obvious exceptions – are also delayed to reflect the credit allowed to the business by its suppliers.

Also, profits are calculated after providing for depreciation – some £90,000 in total. And depreciation is a book allowance rather than a cash payment.

The other side of the coin is that capital expenditure is, or can be, an immediate drain on cash resources. It all depends how the capital spending is financed.

Madeup Turner Trading has decided that it will pay for the first £50,000 of the purchase price of new lathes from its own resources. It will borrow the remaining £150,000. But the managing director's new car will be financed by hire purchase while new computer equipment will be leased.

Detailed calculation

Each of the figures included in the various budget statements will have been built up from a series of estimates. In the case of the sales budget, for example, the quarterly figures would have been built up from individual salespeople's returns, as discussed earlier.

And, wherever possible, calculations will be made and documented based on the obvious mathematical link between figures, as in the case of capital spending and depreciation charges, or all of the cash flow figures and other budget statements.

So the whole is a logical package with mathematical integrity. That, of course, does not mean that it is 'right'. Any one, and probably most, if not all, of the estimations and assumptions used will turn out to have been at least a little wide of the mark. And what is more to the point, the budget represents only one path through the minefield of decisions that must be made.

The next step is to look again at the figures, trying to avoid a few more of those mines.

10. Spotting the weaknesses

Weaknesses can find their way into budgets either by a failure of logic or arithmetical accuracy (some of the calculations have been based on a false premiss or there have been miscalculations) or by way of flawed tactical or strategic decisions. In other words, the plan needs to be refined or changed.

The first and subsequent drafts of budgets provide opportunities to identify those weaknesses and discuss policy options.

In many businesses the best way to do this will be by way of a formal budget review, this time working from the top down, but also involving all those with budgeting responsibility.

Typically, this might involve, say, a management review and a decision to delay installing a new piece of plant. Those responsible for production figures are then asked to work out how this will affect their plans and write the result into a revised budget.

Providing yardsticks

Measurements are only useful against a yardstick. And budgets are no exception.

If budget calculations reveal an expected profit of £100,000, how is a business to judge whether that is good or bad?

The best yardstick would be the maximum profit possible. But that is not known.

So whether they embrace 'zero base budgeting' ideals or not, most businesses are forced to fall back on the best information they have available when reviewing budget figures. And that information is what has gone before.

The review process then becomes one of questioning every line of the budget. Does it make sense within the overall pattern of what is going on? Have key ratios, such as profit margin, been affected? If so, how and why? Are significant increases or decreases from last year explained by the assumptions used, the known facts and the overall plan? Will planned changes lead to better or worse results? Is the overall result satisfactory, even viable?

Back to Madeup Turner Trading

At Madeup Turner Trading (Figures 8.1–8.7) the overall result has taken a dive. Worse still, the crisis looks as if it will deepen towards the end of the year (Figure 8.7).

Previous year figures show first quarter losses about the same as in the previous year, largely owing to seasonal fluctuations in the level of sales to the car trade.

But despite a rising trend of sales during the year, the final quarter will see the company trading at a loss.

Although the new Nuts & bolts contract means lower margins on this product, the overall level of margin looks reasonably satisfactory. But there are three other areas which look worthy of investigation: the continuing losses on Screws, the increase in overheads and the additional finance charges.

A major change

Looking at its overheads first, Madeup Turner Trading accepts that part of the reason for an increase in its administration cost budget (Figure 8.5) – the rise in rent and rates costs – is outside its immediate control. The factory is almost fully utilised and there is no possibility of sub-letting any part. Short of moving, it must accept the increase.

Another reason for the increase is the additional depreciation charge resulting from the planned acquisition of new computer equipment. But the finance director is adamant that this is needed to improve the accounting system and credit control and cash collection, matters vital to maintaining adequate cash flow.

Although small in saving, the replacement of the managing director's car is less vital and it is decided to delay this until the next financial year.

Turning to its sales and marketing budget (Figure 8.4), a big question mark is put over advertising plans. Although the advertising budget has been put up substantially, the gain does not seem obvious.

But more significant changes can be made when it comes to the Screws product line.

Getting down to Nuts & bolts

The budget shows that there will be a negative contribution from Screws of almost £19,000. If this product line were dropped the overheads charge that it currently bears – £21,860, see Figure 8.2 – would have to be re-allocated to Nuts & bolts.

Madeup Turner Trading has been concerned about the problem for some time and had hoped that a substantial price increase would make the Screws product line more viable. It has not turned out that way.

But with its new Nuts & bolts contract it has a chance to make the change.

Although on the face of it the contribution level would be worse, this would not be the case if the lathe used to produce Screws were used instead to produce Nuts & bolts. Only one new lathe would then have to be purchased giving a saving in depreciation and interest costs. Further, the advertising budget, increased in part to back a price hike for Screws, can be slimmed down.

It is decided to discontinue the Screws product line and to revise the budgets accordingly (Figures 10.1–10.7).

Scheduled production	Units (000)	Units (000)	Units (000)	Units (000)	Units (000)
Nuts & bolts	4,700	6,600	8,500	9,600	29,400

			Quarters		
Indirect costs	First £	Second £	Third £	Fourth £	Year £
Depreciation	10,000	10,000	12,500	12,500	45,000
Repairs and maintenance	2,500	2,500	2,650	2,650	10,300
Heat, light and power	8,700	9,000	11,000	11,000	39,700
Indirect wages	7,000	7,000	7,000	7,000	28,000
Total	28,200	28,500	33,150	33,150	123,000

Figure 10.1 *Madeup Turner Trading: production budget – indirect costs*

Nuts & bolts – variable production costs			Quarters		
	First £	Second £	Third £	Fourth £	Year £
Materials	32,430	45,540	87,975	99,360	265,305
Wages	22,560	31,680	47,600	53,760	155,600
Total variable costs	54,990	77,220	135,575	153,120	420,905
Cost per unit	1.17p	1.17p	1.60	1.6p	1.43p
Indirect costs	28,200	28,500	33,150	33,150	123,000
Total costs	83,190	105,720	168,725	186,270	543,905
Cost per unit	1.17	1.60	1.99	1.94	1.85

Nuts & bolts Cost of sales and stock					Quarters			
	First		Second		Third		Fourth	
	Units (000)	Value £	Units (000)	Value £	Units (000)	Value £	Units (000)	Value £
Opening stock	1,200	19,800	2,060	35,960	2,160	35,338	1,100	21,057
Add production	4,700	83,190	6,600	105,720	8,500	168,725	9,600	186,270
Total	5,900	102,990	8,660	141,680	10,660	204,063	10,700	207,327
Less sales	3,840	67,030	6,500	106,342	9,560	183,006	9,640	186,788
Closing stock		35,960	2,160	35,338	1,100	21,057	1,060	20,539
Cost per unit		1.74		1.64		1.91		1.94

Figure 10.2 *Production costs – Nuts & bolts*

	Quarters				
	First £	Second £	Third £	Fourth £	Year £
Salaries	28,000	28,000	32,000	32,000	120,000
Expenses	6,000	9,000	8,000	7,000	30,000
Car depreciation	3,000	3,000	3,000	3,000	12,000
Advertising and promotional literature	2,000	7,000	5,000	10,000	24,000
Total	39,000	47,000	48,000	52,000	186,000
Last year	35,000	45,000	45,000	35,000	160,000
Percentage increase	11.4%	4.4%	6.7%	48.6%	16.25%

Figure 10.3 *Madeup Turner Trading: sales and marketing department costs*

	Quarters				
	First £	Second £	Third £	Fourth £	Year £
Salaries	44,000	44,000	49,000	49,000	186,000
Expenses	2,500	2,500	2,500	2,500	10,000
Postage, printing and stationery	6,000	6,000	6,000	6,000	24,000
Rent and rates	11,000	23,000	23,000	23,000	80,000
Car depreciation	2,000	2,000	2,000	2,000	8,000
Computer depreciation	2,000	2,000	6,000	6,000	16,000
Furniture depreciation	500	500	500	500	2,000
Total	68,000	80,000	89,000	89,000	326,000
Last year	66,000	68,000	69,000	66,000	269,000
Percentage increase	3.0%	17.6%	29.0%	34.8%	21.2%

Figure 10.4 *Madeup Turner Trading: administration department*

	Quarters				
	First £	Second £	Third £	Fourth £	Year £
New lathes (Depreciation rate 10% per annum)	–	–	100,000	–	100,000
Computer equipment (Depreciation rate 25% per annum)	–	–	64,000	–	64,000
Total	–	–	164,000	–	164,000

Figure 10.5 *Madeup Turner Trading: capital expenditure budget*

	First £	Second £	Quarters Third £	Fourth £	Year £
Sales income Nuts & bolts	152,000	253,000	331,000	321,000	1057,000
Production costs Nuts & bolts	67,030	106,342	183,006	186,788	543,166
Contribution	84,970	146,658	147,994	134,212	513,834
Overheads Sales and marketing	39,000	47,000	48,000	52,000	186,000
Administration	68,000	80,000	89,000	89,000	326,000
Total overheads	107,000	127,000	137,000	141,000	512,000
Net contribution	(22,030)	19,658	10,994	(6,788)	1,834
Leasing			2,000	2,000	4,000
Finance charges			1,750	1,750	3,500
			3,750	3,750	7,500
Net profit	(22,030)	19,658	7,244	(10,538)	(5,666)
Last year	(21,400)	9,100	12,700	9,600	10,000

Figure 10.6 *Madeup Turner Trading: trading summary*

Revised budget

By working through its budget Madeup Turner Trading has been able to come up with a revised plan which has cut its expected losses from £34,790 to £4,666 while improving its cash position.

By continuing the process of review, questioning and amendment, it should be able to reach a plan putting it back into profitability.

			Quarters		
	First £	Second £	Third £	Fourth £	Year £
Receipts					
Sales	232,200	178,400	297,400	386,500	1094,500
Bank loan		75,000			75,000
Total	232,200	253,400	297,400	386,500	1169,500
Payments					
Productions costs					
Fixed costs:					
Repairs and maintenance	2,900	2,900	2,900	3,300	12,000
Heat, light and power	10,200	10,200	10,500	12,100	43,000
Wages	7,000	7,000	7,000	7,000	28,000
Variable:	55,000	59,000	81,500	143,500	339,000
Sales and marketing	33,500	37,800	46,400	47,500	165,200
Administration	73,800	75,500	76,800	80,700	306,800
VAT	18,225	4,375	23,300	31,300	77,200
Capital expenditure:					
Lathes	29,375	88,125			117,500
Loan repayments			3,750	3,750	7,500
Leasing					
Computer equipment		8,000	2,000	2,000	12,000
Finance charges			1,750	1,750	3,500
Total	230,000	292,900	255,900	332,900	1110,700
Balance brought forward	83,000	85,200	45,700	87,200	83,000
Add receipts	232,200	253,400	297,400	386,500	1169,500
Less payments	315,200	338,600	343,100	473,700	1252,500
	230,000	292,900	255,900	332,900	1111,700
Balance carried forward	85,200	45,700	87,200	140,800	140,800

Figure 10.7 *Madeup Turner Trading: cash flow statements*

11. What next?

The budgetary process does not end with the agreement of a satisfactory plan for next year. Part of the purpose of the exercise is to plot a course that promises success.

But no matter how accurate the chart, no matter how precise the pencil line that shows the way, the desired destination will not be reached unless progress along that line is checked frequently and steering adjustments made when necessary.

Comparisons between budgets and actual results reveal leeway and drift.

Just as budgets represent a logical and coordinated picture of expected results, so management accounts provide a coordinated view of what has actually happened.

Differences between the two can therefore be explained by a process of reasoning and analysis. This exercise should be undertaken.

First, it will help managers to learn more about their business and the effect of the decisions they have taken. Second, it will identify where things have not gone according to plan and where correcting action needs to be taken.

Businesses may never succeed in making their budgets, but carefully prepared and closely monitored budgets will enable managers to keep their business pointing in the direction of the goals they have set themselves.

	Quarter			Year to date		
	Actual £	*Budget* £	*Variance* %	*Actual* £	*Budget* £	*Variance* %
Sales						
Units (000)	7,500	6,500	15.4	11,400	10,340	10.3
Price per unit	3.86	3.9	(1.0)	3.8	3.9	(2.6)
Value	289,600	253,000	14.5	433,200	405,000	7.0
Production costs						
Nuts & bolts	122,300	106,342	(15.0)	186,400	173,372	(7.5)
Contribution	167,300	146,658	14.1	246,800	231,628	6.6
Overheads						
Sales and marketing	45,000	47,000	4.3	88,000	86,000	(2.3)
Administration	83,500	80,000	(4.4)	150,000	148,000	(1.4)
Total overheads	128,500	127,000	(1.2)	238,000	234,000	(1.7)
Net contribution	38,800	19,658	97.4	8,800	(2,372)	
Leasing						
Finance charges						
Net profit	38,800	19,658	97.4	8,800	(2,372)	

Madeup Turner Trading finds that its actual results exceed its budget figures by some margin. Analysis shows that this is largely owing to higher than expected sales – at slightly reduced prices. Estimates of production costs (per unit) and overheads have proved reasonably accurate. So Madeup Turner Trading managers must decide whether production capacity is sufficient to meet increased demand and/or whether it would be advisable to adjust selling prices.

Figure 11.1 *Madeup Turner Trading: management accounts, second quarter*

12. How do you measure up?

Running a business efficiently means making the most of resources and the least of wastage. The principle applies equally to money, machinery, materials, manpower and systems.

So it makes no sense to have control systems that are too sophisticated. Collecting more information than can be used is wasteful. Spending more on checks than is likely to be saved does not help the cash position – it makes it worse.

Precisely what each business does to make sure that it is making the most of its chances is therefore down to managerial judgement; there are no hard and fast rules. A shipbuilder is bound to have different problems and different priorities from a tobacconist, for example.

Even so, there are broad areas where every business should have considered the problems faced, the opportunities and pitfalls, and have decided upon a policy – even if that policy is to do nothing.

Below are the major headings that should feature in budgeting strategy.

Accounting

Accounting must be up to the task. It must be sophisticated enough to provide up-to-date information on income and expenditure, debtors and creditors, and the cash position – as speedily and frequently as deemed necessary. Above all, the accounting system should serve the business and not drive it.

Accounting arrangements should incorporate a suitable degree of internal control to avoid wastage, mistakes and fraud. They should include regular cash reconciliations between bank and cash book figures. They should ensure that invoices and statements are accurate and issued in good time and that money received is banked without delay.

Budgetary control

Any business of any size needs budgets – an expression of expectations that is used for planning and useful in judging performance. Frequency of time breaks and degree of detail will depend upon the size and type of business. But budgets should certainly encompass trading expectations and cash flow in the form of a cash flow statement.

Nor is budgeting a once-a-year exercise. Budgets should be monitored and updated on a regular basis to reflect significant changes of plan or circumstance.

Capital expenditure

Timing and amount of capital expenditure is usually optional to some degree. It should not be entered into without the likelihood of benefit to the business, availability of longer-term finance and certainty that cash outflow can be met.

In essence this calls for some form of investment appraisal and for capital expenditure plans to be written into the cash flow statement.

Cash

There should be a means of ensuring that cash held in bank accounts which pay little or no interest, and for that matter in petty cash tins, is kept to a minimum. Maximising cash flow is not about having the largest possible bank balance. It is about making sure cash that is used in the best possible way – and that means earning for the business.

Credit control

Every business should have a credit control policy covering vetting, credit limits, terms of trade, documentation, monitoring, chasing, dealing with queries, and bad debts.

There should be firm guidelines on the procedures to follow before anybody is allowed credit. Usually, these will call for some form of prior checking by, for example, asking for credit references.

Credit limits should usually be set for each customer and terms of trade agreed, confirmed and recorded. Policy should set out action to be undertaken if credit limits or terms are breached. Salespeople should know the degree of flexibility in credit terms, if any, on which they are permitted to negotiate and whether cash discounts are offered for early payment.

Invoicing should be swift and accurate, and supported by statements of account issued at regular intervals and setting out total indebtedness.

Outstanding debtors should be monitored constantly and overdue accounts identified. There should be known procedures for chasing overdue debts. Queries raised during this process must be answered quickly.

Finally, there should be a policy covering when and how legal or other recovery procedures are commenced, and at what point, and on whose authority debts are declared bad and written off. There should be a system for ensuring that VAT on bad debts is recovered and not forgotten.

Debtors

Steps should be taken to gain the best possible credit terms with suppliers. This will entail building up a strong balance sheet so that your credit rating is good, building up a reputation for paying on due dates, and making sure that credit terms are always included in purchase negotiations.

Long-term finance

Cash flow will always be in jeopardy if the business does not have sufficient long-term capital.

Businesses must start with sufficient capital, borrow sufficient long-term amounts, and retain sufficient profits to ensure a strong balance sheet. In particular, capital expenditure should be financed from longer-term sources and, in nearly every circumstance, current assets should always outstrip current liabilities.

Gearing should not be allowed to get out of hand so that the long-term borrowing element of capital employed – as opposed to equity capital and retained profits – becomes a burden to the extent that interest or scheduled capital repayments cannot be met.

Monitoring

Performance should be monitored constantly to identify opportunities, weaknesses, problems and variations from plan. This means systematic and regular comparison of actual results with budgeted results – including cash flow figures – and probably the use of selected ratios.

Use of assets should also be monitored on a regular basis so that under-utilised furniture, equipment, premises or vehicles can be either put to alternative and better use or sold off or rented out to realise cash.

Revenue expenditure

There should be proper control of revenue expenditure in terms of both budgeting and authorisation. Only selected individuals should be entitled to commit the business to expenditure and then only within previously agreed plans or criteria.

Controls should be designed to cut out waste, ensure best prices and efficient buying, and avoid over-stocking.

Petty cash too should be controlled with permitted expenditure and authorisation levels for expenses and other items set and made known to all concerned.

Stock control

Every effort should be made to keep stock levels to the very minimum necessary to trade effectively. In a manufacturing business product design will have a bearing on stock levels. In all businesses marketing policy will have an impact. There should be a means of assessing the cost of holding stock and the savings available by, for example, standardising components or limiting product ranges.

Target stock levels and reordering criteria should be in place for each raw material or finished item which a business decides to stock. These levels should take into account stockholding costs, likely future availability and delivery periods, and expected price movements.

Work in progress should also be monitored and kept to a minimum through efficient scheduling and control and management of delaying factors.

Glossary

Absorption or full cost accounting: The notion that prices should be set at a level that will cover both direct and an appropriate proportion of indirect costs. Where, as is usually the case, a number of product lines are involved, this means deciding upon a 'fair' allocation of indirect costs.

Accruals: Provisions set aside for amounts known to be owing but not yet invoiced by the supplier – as, for example, electricity used since the last bill was received.

Balance sheet: A financial statement showing the book values of what a business owes and what it owns at that moment, differentiating between long-term finance, fixed assets, current liabilities and current assets.

Break-even point: The point, measured in units sold, at which sales revenue covers both fixed and variable costs.

Budget: A financial statement setting out the best estimate of the outcome of trading in a future period. Separate budgets can be prepared to cover various aspects of trading.

Capital employed: Money invested in a business over the long term and including owners' capital (share capital in the case of a limited company), retained profits and long-term loans.

Capital expenditure: The cost of acquiring assets *used in* a business rather than *used up* (the latter being revenue expenditure). Purchases of land, buildings, machinery and vehicles are examples of capital expenditure.

Cash flow: Net of cash receipts and cash payments in a period.

Cash flow statement: A statement setting out the expected inflows and outflows of cash over a future trading period and showing the current best estimate of movements that will occur in the bank balance.

Cost centre: An element of the overall budget – and hence a management responsibility – that deals with level of expenditure only.

Creditors: All those to whom a business owes money.

Debtors: All those who owe a business money.

Depreciation: Notional charge against profits for the use of fixed assets.

Direct costs: Costs which can be directly attributed to a particular product. Direct costs tend to be variable costs but, depending upon the nature of the business and its organisation, are not necessarily so.

Discounted cash flow: Expected future net receipts adjusted to take account of their timing and of interest costs to give an indication of present value.

Financial accounts: Year end financial statements prepared, in the case of companies, in accordance with the requirements of the Companies Act and accounting standards drawn up by the Accounting Standards Board. Company year end financial accounts must be audited by a registered auditor who is required to say whether, in his opinion, they represent a 'true and fair view' of results and position.

Fixed assets: Those assets such as premises, plant, equipment and vehicles used in the business. In general fixed assets are kept for their useful working life and are not expected to be sold to realise cash in the short term.

Fixed costs: Those business costs which tend not to vary in line with different levels of trading. Thus in the short term rent paid for a factory site is likely to remain fixed whether working at 80 per cent capacity or 95 per cent capacity.

Flexible budgeting: The system of frequent or continual updating of budgets to reflect changes in levels of trading.

Indirect costs: Those costs which cannot be attributed directly to product lines and which therefore do not vary in direct proportion to production or sales.

Investment appraisal: Means of assessing the financial worth of investing in fixed assets.

Limited company: A legally incorporated business having a separate identity from its owners who have the protection of limited liability.

Management accounts: Accounts prepared to enable management to monitor the performance of their business. There is no legal requirement to produce such accounts and no standard format, each business being free to devise the form of reporting best suited to its situation.

Marginal costing: A way of looking at costing and pricing policy in terms of the margin that can be achieved over direct costs only without attempting arbitrary allocation of indirect costs to particular product lines. Sometimes used as a justification for reducing prices, the idea being that some contribution to overheads is better than none.

Matching concept: Sometimes called 'accruals accounting', matching is used in the calculation of profits so that costs are matched against the revenue they generate irrespective of when cash changes hands.

Overheads: Those costs which cannot be directly or individually attributed to products or departments. Hence an accounts department might be deemed an overhead. In budgets with more than one profit centre overheads are allocated between centres according to agreed but probably arbitrary rules.

Partnership: A business owned and run by two or more people who share profits and also responsibility for its debts.

Pay-back period: The time it takes a fixed asset investment to recuperate its own cost.

Profit: There are many definitions of profit, one of the broadest being the increase in value of a business over a given period.

Profits can include both trading profits and capital profits (profits from the sale of fixed assets and investments), and can be realised or unrealised.

Profit and loss account: A financial statement showing the results of a business arising during a particular trading period. Credit is taken for sales as and when invoiced which means that no differentiation is made between realised profits (those already turned into cash) and unrealised profits (those yet to be turned into cash).

Profit centre: An element of the overall budget with brings in both revenue and expenditure and places responsibility for achieving a certain level of contribution.

Profit margin: The difference between selling price and cost. Gross profit margin, not taking into account overhead costs, is an equivalent to 'mark-up' for retailers.

Return on capital: Profit as a percentage of capital employed (or net assets, which come to the same total). Return on capital is an overall indication of business performance and can be compared with current interest rates which show the return on capital from risk-free investment of money in an interest-bearing account.

Revenue expenditure: Spending on consumables such as raw materials, heat, power and light, and labour costs – items used up in the business process.

Sensitivity analysis: Assessment of the vulnerability of the business to the uncertainties inherent in key figures.

Standard costing: The practice of arriving at a 'standard cost' for each item produced. The total theoretical cost of products sold can therefore be calculated by reference to standard costs and any variances from actual costs analysed by cause; for example, because of variances in volume of production, in product mix or raw material prices.

Trade creditors: All those who are owed money as a result of trading with the business – usually by providing goods or services on credit.

Trade debtors: All those owing a business money as the result of trading with it – usually buying goods or services on credit.

Trading profit: That part of profit derived from normal and continuing trading activities and excluding capital profits and other extraordinary items.

Value Added Tax: A tax on consumers by way of a levy on goods and services. Traders act as collectors by charging VAT on invoices and paying over such amounts, less the VAT they have paid to suppliers, to Customs and Excise. VAT does not affect the profits of VAT-registered traders but does affect their cash flow.

Variable costs: Those costs which increase or decrease in direct line with the volume of business undertaken. Material costs are an example.

What if analysis: Reworking figures on the basis of different underlying key assumptions so as to reveal risks and opportunities.

Work in progress: The value of part completed production before it becomes finished stock. Work in progress forms part of working capital.

Zero base budgeting: The notion that budgeting doesn't start from here. Budget setting must be approached with an open mind not inhibited by the figures set last year.

www. DsA. gov.uk.

3 PRINCIPLES OF EXTERNAL QUALITY ASSURANCE

Introduction

External quality assurance relates to the monitoring of training, assessment and internal quality assurance processes and practices in an education or training organisation. The process seeks to ensure that assessment and internal quality assurance activities have been conducted in a consistent, safe and fair manner, in line with relevant requirements, regulations and standards. If you are an internal quality assurer, but not yet an external quality assurer, the content of this chapter will help you understand how you will be monitored and supported in your role.

This chapter will explore the role of an external quality assurer, along with the concepts and principles which underpin it.

This chapter will cover the following topics:

- External quality assurance
- Roles and responsibilities of an external quality assurer
- Concepts and principles of external quality assurance
- Risk management
- The role of technology in external quality assurance

External quality assurance

External quality assurance (EQA) activities should take place on behalf of an awarding organisation (AO) to ensure the learners who have been registered with them have received a quality service. Learners will be working towards a qualification in an education, training or employment organisation known as a centre, which has been approved by an AO. There are many AOs, and centres are free to choose who they work with. If a centre is not happy with the service they receive from the AO or the external quality assurer (EQA), they could choose to go elsewhere.

Any organisation can become an approved centre, for example, colleges, charities, public, private and voluntary organisations, businesses or prisons, providing they meet the qualification and the AO's requirements. However, some training providers might offer in-house programmes of learning to their staff and not be an approved centre with an AO. They might therefore appoint a person to act like an EQA to monitor the assessment and internal

- completing the EQA report online, or offline and uploading it later

- observing live assessment activities via an online visual communication program

- partaking in video conferencing and webinars, for example, AO updates and standardisation activities

- using e-mails with integrated video facilities to send visual messages, as well as attaching documents and images

- using electronic record keeping, i.e. saving documents in the cloud or to the AO's intranet using web conferencing to talk to assessors, IQAs, learners and witnesses if they are quite a distance away.

There are various advantages and limitations to learners, trainers, assessors, IQAs and yourself as an EQA. Having some knowledge of this will help you support your centres.

Table 3.2 Advantages and limitations of using technology

Advantages	Limitations
• accessible and inclusive • addresses sustainability, i.e. no need for paper copies • an efficient use of time and cost-effective, i.e. eliminates time taken to travel to individual assessment sites • auditable and reliable • available, i.e. resources and materials can be accessed at a time and place to suit • gives immediate results from online tests • learners can 'bring your own device' (BYOD) to use during sessions • on demand, i.e. tests can be taken when a learner is ready	• finance is required to purchase or upgrade equipment • it can lead to plagiarism by learners • it is time consuming to initially set up • it might create barriers if someone cannot access it or is not confident to use it • learners/assessors accessing the internet via their own devices might run out of credit • power cuts/low broadband speeds/limited wifi network • security of data could be compromised • some people might be afraid of using new technology • some organisations block access to certain sites and social media • there might not be enough resources available for all learners to use at the same time (if part of group work)

If you are monitoring the decisions of centre staff which have been made based on electronic learner evidence, you need to be sure the work does belong to them. The assessor should have confirmed the identity of the learner, and the learner should sign an authenticity statement to validate the work is theirs. You will need to find out what system the centre uses to check the identification of their assessors as well as their learners.

You might need to check with the centre in advance as to what online systems they are using, how the assessment and IQA processes are used, and how they ensure authenticity. Many qualifications and programmes are delivered online, some may have hundreds of

☐ *Agree relevant action points and appropriate target dates, along with any improvement points for guidance.*

☐ *Give constructive and developmental feedback to staff, and allow time for their questions.*

☐ *Explain how the centre will receive the report and when, and when the next monitoring activity will be carried out.*

Remote monitoring activity

This activity is to sample learners' work, assessment and internal quality assurance documents without having to visit the centre. When you plan to carry out a remote monitoring activity, you must be very clear about what you wish to sample, as you may not have the opportunity to ask for additional documents on the day. If you do need to carry out a more detailed sample, you will need to arrange another date when the centre can get this information to you. However, if you are accessing the information and documents electronically, you might be able to carry out an additional sample if necessary. Always ensure you have been given any relevant passwords and guidance as to how to access a centre's online system.

There are also other issues with a remote monitoring activity, such as the sample not arriving by the due date, the package being left with a neighbour who has since gone out, misunderstandings regarding what was asked for and items getting lost in the post. Electronic access may therefore make the process easier and rule out problems with using postal services if the centre operates this way.

Activities you could carry out during a remote monitoring activity include:

● sampling learner work which has been assessed formatively and summatively by different assessors, and which has and has not been internally quality assured

● sampling assessment and IQA decisions and feedback records

● sampling minutes of meetings, standardisation records, appeals and complaints, initial and diagnostic assessment results, interview and induction records, tutorial review records, analyses of evaluations and questionnaires

● using the telephone and/or internet for communicating with staff and learners.

Example

Annabelle, the external quality assurer, was completing a remote monitoring activity at home and noticed that the units she had requested from the centre had not been provided. She also noticed there were no internal quality assurance records. She telephoned the centre contact who explained that they had substituted the learners' work due to absences. They also said the internal quality assurer had gone on holiday and not left his records behind. This gave Annabelle

(Continued)

However, it could be that during a monitoring activity you find something very serious, for example, plagiarism, malpractice or fraud. Your AO should have given you training regarding what to do in situations like this. This should involve you making a phone call to your contact at the AO in the first instance, without alerting the centre to what you have found. If you are in the centre at the time, you could tell your centre contact you need some fresh air and go outside to make a discreet phone call. You might be told to place the centre on a sanction and to agree a detailed action plan before leaving. However, once the AO receives your report, they have the final say on what sanction a centre will be placed.

It's best to be proactive and keep in touch with your centres between monitoring activities, encouraging them to communicate any concerns or issues they may have. This will enable you to support them, to be proactive and not reactive when something more serious occurs.

Extension activity

Reflect upon your most recent visit to a centre. Were you happy with the way it went? Did you remain professional or did you get too friendly with the staff? Did you find anything wrong and have to give an action point? If so, were you able to back this up by showing the centre staff the written requirements? What would you have done differently if you had the chance?

Providing feedback to centre staff

Feedback should be given throughout the sampling process during a visit, for example, after an observation of an assessor, as well as at the end of the visit. If you are carrying out a remote monitoring activity, you could telephone the centre part way through if you have any queries. Feedback should only be based on what was sampled and monitored. It can be used to confirm compliance and competence, and to motivate and encourage centre staff. It can also be used to highlight areas for improvement, development and action.

You should give ongoing feedback at each opportunity; this can highlight good practice and be used as a basis to discuss any areas for concern. Pontin (2012: 156) states: *The EQA will often give informal verbal feedback throughout the day, and this should be helpful to the centre as it means that there will be no 'nasty surprises' during the formal feedback at the closing meeting. However, it is important that even this informal feedback is captured on the report as otherwise it is likely to be forgotten or overlooked by all parties.*

Always remain professional when giving feedback and ensure you have valid evidence regarding what you have seen and any action points you have identified. At all times, remain objective and do not let any personal factors influence your decisions.

Please see Chapter 2 for information regarding different feedback methods such as evaluative or descriptive, constructive or destructive, and objective or subjective.

Identifying and allocating responsibilities to team members

Once you know who your team members are, along with their skills, knowledge and experience, you can begin allocating various activities to them to meet the objectives. You will firstly need to identify and make a list of all the activities you expect yourself and your team members to carry out. You can then create a work plan for yourself and other plans for relevant team members.

Wherever possible, you should delegate tasks to your team members based upon their strengths. It could be that you plan a yearly calendar of team meetings and prepare the agendas, but not chair them all. Delegating some meetings to other team members on a rota basis will give them responsibility and help them take ownership of agreed actions. You could ask your team members to carry out a SWOT analysis to assist this process. SWOT stands for **s**trengths, **w**eaknesses, **o**pportunities and **t**hreats. It's also useful to carry out a SWOT analysis yourself.

Strengths and weaknesses can be considered as internal (i.e. within the organisation) whereas opportunities and threats can be considered as external (outside of the organisation). Strengths and opportunities can be helpful, whereas weaknesses and threats can be harmful. A SWOT analysis is useful for identifying an individual's strengths and weaknesses, as well as the opportunities available and the threats faced. A swot analysis can be used for products, services and projects, as well as for people, to identify favourable and unfavourable contributing factors.

Activity

Think of your own role at this moment in time, and complete the SWOT boxes below. Once completed, what do you think you need to do as a result? You could ask your team members to complete one too.

	Helpful	**Harmful**
Internal	*Strengths*	*Weaknesses*
External	*Opportunities*	*Threats*

Carrying out a SWOT analysis is fine for finding things out, but you need to do something with the results. Listing strengths and weakness, while identifying opportunities and threats, is of no use if you don't use them for a reason. You will need to decide what that reason is, and whether it's for yourself and/or your team members. Once identified, you will need to apply the strengths and take advantage of the opportunities. You will also need to minimise

APPENDIX

Abbreviations and acronyms

AAIA	Association for Achievement and Improvement through Assessment
AAO	Approved Assessment Organisation
ACL	Adult and Community Learning
ADD	Attention Deficit Disorder
ADHD	Attention Deficit and Hyperactivity Disorder
ADS	Adult Dyslexia Support
AELP	Association of Employment and Learning Providers
AI	Awarding Institution
AO	Awarding Organisation
AoC	Association of Colleges
ASD	Autism Spectrum Disorder
ATL	Association of Teachers and Lecturers
BEd	Bachelor of Education
BIS	Department for Business, Innovation and Skills
BKSB	Basic Key Skills Builder
BYOD	Bring Your Own Device
CCEA	Council for the Curriculum, Examinations and Assessment (Northern Ireland)
CETT	Centre for Excellence in Teacher Training
Cert Ed	Certificate in Education
CIEA	Chartered Institute for Educational Assessors
CIF	Common Inspection Framework
CL	Community Learning
CLA	Copyright Licensing Authority
COSHH	Control of Substances Hazardous to Health
CPD	Continuing Professional Development